20.V.50

# THREE TALES OF HAMLET

# THREE TALES OF HAMLET

by

## RAYNER HEPPENSTALL

and

## MICHAEL INNES

LONDON
VICTOR GOLLANCZ LTD
1950

*Copyright 1950 by Rayner Heppenstall and J. I. M. Stewart*

*Printed in Great Britain by*
*The Camelot Press Ltd., London and Southampton*

# CONTENTS

# CONTENTS

# PREFACE

THE CONTENTS OF this book are the texts of three
entertainments devised for the B.B.C.'s Third Programme, two of them in dramatic form and one a highly
mannered talk delivered by its author. The two dramatic
scripts are prefaced by observations previously offered in
part to readers of the *Radio Times*, though most of what
is said about "The Fool's Saga" was at first intended for
an introductory talk which in fact never took place. The
various pieces have more in common than their devotion
to Shakespeare's enigmatical tragedy.

The first of two series of Imaginary Conversations
which I undertook to edit and produce in 1946 included,
among pieces cut more directly after the Landor pattern,
two in which Hamlet figured. One was a study of
Ophelia's madness by G. W. Stonier, the other a debate
by Herbert Read between Hamlet and the captain of
the pirates who so conveniently abridged the plot for
Shakespeare. "The Hawk and the Handsaw" was commissioned for the second series. It outgrew itself and
became what it is, with a large cast and music for a full
orchestra. "The Mysterious Affair at Elsinore" was
abridged for broadcasting from a paper read to the
Oxford English Society. I wrote "The Fool's Saga"
because I had so much enjoyed producing "The Hawk
and the Handsaw." "The Hawk and the Handsaw" was,
from the point of view of radio production, extremely
complicated. It amused me to make "The Fool's Saga"
even more so. Michael Innes now threatens to write me
"something really stratified." As a matter of fact, given
the amount of rehearsal time a B.B.C. producer can

normally afford, "The Fool's Saga" was too complicated. A number of listeners were confused. As a production, I am forced to the conclusion that it was a failure.

Perhaps this justifies its publication. There is a school of professional thought which holds that writing for radio is wholly *sui generis*, and that the better a script the less well it will read. I do not agree with this, and I think that any kind of good writing will broadcast well if the appropriate means are found. I defy, for instance, anybody to say that Hamlet's final apologia on p. 69 is not a piece of excellent prose or that, ringingly delivered by Cyril Cusack, it was not equally a piece of "good radio." There are, nevertheless, specific uses of the blind, audible medium which cannot easily be transposed to the printed page. The first series of Imaginary Conversations appeared in a book and were received very kindly by the critical Press. They, however, began with a pattern set in print and used few tricks of presentation. Here, it is different.

As to the content of these two longer pieces, I did not myself perceive the closest link between them until, on the eve of producing "The Fool's Saga," I read the chapters on the saga Hamlet in Ernest Jones's *Hamlet and Œdipus*. To this figure of legend, Dr. Jones wishes to apply the same Freudian analysis as both Michael Innes and he apply to Shakespeare's sweet prince. This does not seem to me to be reasonable. Just as the theories of Karl Marx become less and less convincing as you apply them to societies remote from nineteenth-century capitalism, so, as it seems to me, does the Œdipus complex diminish in applicability the further you get from those Victorian fathers. It is true that Œdipus was not himself a Victorian, but it is not improbable that Greek society also had its phase of unbridled patriarchy, and not until

8

the nineteenth century was the prototypical force either of this myth or of Shakespeare's tragedy at all widely felt.

The extraordinary thing is that the game of mothers and fathers had reached a crisis of quite a different kind in what historians call the period of migrations. The Picts (Saxo's Hamlet bigamously marries a Pictish queen) seem to have clung to matrilineal succession and the exogamic selection of husbands longer than any other people in Europe (it was Lady Macbeth who had a claim to the Scottish throne). But elsewhere too a happy issue to the war between men and women had yet to be reached.

In matriarchal societies, a boy's hatred of his father cannot be so intense. In many cases, the father's possession of the mother began and ended with the child's conception, and the male head of the family is commonly an uncle. The fact that Saxo's Hamlet slew one uncle and was later slain by another is to Dr. Jones evidence of the fabulist's hypocrisy (a collective fabulist's unconscious hypocrisy, it goes without saying). To him, an uncle is simply a father-substitute. Is this not arbitrarily to blur the outlines of the story? To Dr. Jones, it would similarly be a matter of indifference whether Kemp Malone was right in supposing the girl I call "Thora" to have been Hamlet's sister. Foster-sister, sister, first cousin, the girl next door—they are all mother-substitutes to him.

The relevance of all this to the understanding of Shakespeare lies, I suggest, in the fact that England in Shakespeare's day was ruled by a Virgin Queen about whom mythical attributes clustered even in her lifetime. Matriarchy was, so to speak, in the air. It is odd that Robert Graves, who, in *The White Goddess*, if I have understood it, pleads for the restoration of matriarchal principles on the ground that it would be good for poets, should have failed to insist on the matriarchal character of our golden age in poetry. Odd, too, that Mr. Graves's *King Jesus,* which he quotes in another connection, should not have provided Dr. Jones with the clue he needed. Even *The Golden Bough* brought Hamlet's Pictish queen into court when exogamy was the matter under consideration.

**R. H.**

# THE HAWK AND THE HANDSAW

## *by* Michael Innes

First broadcast on Sunday, November 21st, 1948, with the following cast:

| | |
|---|---|
| Doctor Mungo | JOHN LAURIE |
| His Boy | DENISE BRYER |
| Horatio | FREDERICK LLOYD |
| King Fortinbras | BALIOL HOLLOWAY |
| Hamlet | CYRIL CUSACK |
| A Girl | HILDA SCHRODER |
| 1st Player ("Hamlet") | LAIDMAN BROWNE |
| 2nd Player ("Horatio") | STANLEY GROOME |
| 3rd Player ("Fortinbras") | WILLIAM TRENT |

The music was composed by William Wordsworth and played by the B.B.C. Theatre Orchestra under Walter Goehr.

# INTRODUCTION

THE FIRST MAN to subject the story of *Hamlet* to severe intellectual scrutiny was Prince Hamlet himself. He had all too abundantly the power to think precisely on an event, and at the crisis of his fortunes the only plan of any complexity that he succeeded in carrying through was clearly the issue of a burdensome doubt. On the battlements of Elsinore the spirit of his father, King Hamlet, had appeared to him and told the story of a strange and unnatural crime. It was untrue that the king had died, as was given out, from the bite of an adder. He had been poisoned by his brother Claudius— the man whose usurping of the throne, and hasty marriage to Hamlet's mother, the widowed queen, had already cast the young prince into deep dejection. Here was a dreadful disclosure. But—Hamlet came to ask himself—was the apparition that made it indeed his father's ghost? As a test he planned his "mouse-trap," a scheme for the playing before Claudius of an old tragedy, *The Murder of Gonzago*, the action of which happened to correspond with the crime supernaturally revealed to him. And when Claudius on witnessing the play showed perturbation and displeasure, Hamlet took this as tantamount to an admission of guilt and a vindication of the ghost's veracity.

Now, what made Hamlet distrustful in the first place was his acquaintance with an important medieval science, that of demonology, for he had learnt from this that a devil may take on the form of a human being, living or dead, in order to lure some other human being into mortal sin—and thus the possibility that the ghost

13

might be *dishonest* had to be reckoned with. But Hamlet was untroubled by another possibility: *that there had been no ghost at all.* This suggestion, with which the more modern science of psychology might have confronted him, was first advanced with any force by an eminent living Elizabethan scholar, Dr. W. W. Greg, in a paper called "Hamlet's Hallucination"—a *tour de force* equalled in its field only by Maurice Morgann's famous essay on Sir John Falstaff. *Why*, Greg asks, that unlikely correspondence between the disclosure of the "ghost" and an old play long familiar to Hamlet? Simply this: that the latter prompts the former! Hamlet, already in great agony of spirit, and swayed by the superstitious imaginings of nervous sentinels, feeds his own obscure suspicions by projecting upon some mere nocturnal vapour both the form of his dead father and the murky old Italian tale that has long haunted his unconscious mind. The apparition, in fact, is not the cause, but a consequence, of his disordered intellect.

In the thirty years since Dr. Greg disturbed the learned with this theory there has been much "psychological" interpretation of Hamlet's story. Most startling, perhaps, is the psycho-analytical view, put forward glancingly by Freud himself and later (with a brilliant command over the whole field of *Hamlet* criticism) by Dr. Ernest Jones. Roughly, we are told that Claudius, in killing Hamlet's father and marrying his mother, has done very much what Hamlet himself as a child unconsciously wanted to do. And this correspondence, although it never comes to conscious focus in the mature man, is sufficiently active at some subliminal level to pop in between Hamlet and his revenge. In a sense he identifies himself with the villain Claudius, and he is thus inhibited from striking at him.

Such attempts as these at plucking out the heart of

Hamlet's mystery have greatly influenced modern Shakespeare criticism. How, we may wonder, would they have influenced Hamlet? Would they have helped him to resolve his perplexities, or would he have found in these rationalising speculations only a further prompting to doubt and hesitation? To these questions "The Hawk and the Handsaw" attempts to sketch an answer in dramatic form.

In such a venture a certain anachronism is bound to peep through the arras of the dialogue, however carefully this be embroidered in an Elizabethan taste. But the effect, I hope, will not be too fantastic, since my medieval doctor has taken only general notions from his modern colleagues; and since, moreover, much of the psychological knowledge that was first systematised by scientists of our own day lay by no means entirely beyond the scope of human conjecture in the age of Montaigne.

Coleridge after reading *The Comedy of Errors* remarked acutely that improbabilities buttress each other. "The Hawk and the Handsaw" brings a second anachronism to the support of the first, and the action, placed in the Danish court some forty years after Hamlet's death, is precipitated by a performance there of *Hamlet, Prince of Denmark*. I must plead that the Hamlet we all vividly know (but who is so mysteriously elusive, nevertheless) is no shadowy figure from the Heroic Age. He is at once Shakespeare's contemporary and our own.

# THE HAWK AND THE HANDSAW

[*A turret chamber giving upon the battlements of Elsinore. Outside, the night is stormy and dark, and there is first heard the various operation of the wind as it sweeps over and through the castle. To this is joined the occasional cry of a gull and the steady wash of the sea. Intermittently, as the stronger waves penetrate farther beneath the cliff, a deeper resonance accompanies their breaking, and the effect is as of a monosyllabic but sustained ejaculation by some deep-toned human voice. There is also distinguishable the dry crackle of a small fire.*

DOCTOR: Do they hold me now of so small account in Denmark that I must nest with martins in this dizzying coign? Feed the fire, boy, and trim that smoking taper. Let me see. So far had I read . . . and so far (*rustle of pages*) . . . ah! (*Reads*) "The ayre meet for melancholicke folke, ought to be thinne, pure and subtile, open and patent to all winds." Open and patent to all winds! Then what a rare purge for melancholy ought this accursed turret-chamber to be. But my affliction is age, boy; age, and a salt rheum, and a calcareous concretion——

BOY: Do you read in the new treatise out of England, sir?

DOCTOR: *A Treatise of Melancholie*, by Timothy Bright, Doctor of Phisicke—the subject my own especial study once. . . . How this Boreal blast pierces the threadbare gown of a discarded man! You serve one, sirrah, to whom was erstwhile brought every ague and distemperature among the great of Denmark. But now the court runs after none but the new doctors, Lopez and Martino. Doctors, indeed! Quacksalvers rather, empirics, rascally and Hermetical knaves, whoreson compounders of foul draughts and noxious——

Boy: Pray, sir, what is your censure of Master Bright's book?

Doctor: Ah, there's a man! A discourse most full and pregnant. Mark! (*Reads*) "The perturbations of melancholy are for the most parte sadde and fearfull, and such as rise of them: as distrust, doubt, diffidence, or dispaire, sometimes furious, and sometimes merry in appearance, through a kind of Sardonian and false laughter. Sometime it falleth out that melancholy men are found verie wittie, and quickly discerne." There Master Bright speaks well.

Boy: May I read, sir! It says that these sick men are given to fearful and terrible dreams.

Doctor: Aye, boy, and their dreams are like a book in which one may read their story. I have treated many such.

Boy (*reads*): "Melancholick humour counterfetteth terrible obiects to the fantasie, and polluting both the substance and spirit of the brayne, causeth it without external occasion to forge monstrous fictions."

Doctor: Even so, even so! And such is the engendering of all hobgoblins and trolls and devils.

BOY (*shocked*): Of *all* devils!

DOCTOR: Yes, I say! Read on.

BOY (*reads*): "This, taking holde of the brayne, by processe of time giueth it an habit of depraued conceite, whereby it fancieth not according to truth; but, as the nature of that humour leadeth it, altogether gastely and fearefull. Fantasie forgeth disguised shapes, which giue great terror vnto the heart——"

[*The chamber door is burst open by the wind, and from below there rises a hum of many voices, with which are mingled the sounds of a Noise of Music tuning up and the stir of a company assembling.*

VOICE OF A GENTLEMAN USHER: The Lord Chamberlain Horatio!

HORATIO (*as if entering the hall hurriedly*): Rise, my lords. His majesty is pleased to grace this trifling entertainment. Rise, my lords and ladies!

BOY: The play!

[*A fanfare of trumpets is followed by a diversity of voices raised in conventional rather than enthusiastic acclamation; from amid this the voice of* KING FORTINBRAS OF DENMARK *emerges.*

VOICES: The king . . . God save your majesty . . . Our humble duty to your majesty . . .

FORTINBRAS: We thank you, your excellencies, my lords and ladies. Pray sit and see this play.

[*The company is heard to settle again amid a subdued murmur which remains as a background to the immediately succeeding speeches.*

BOY: The latch has fallen away, sir. The woodwork's rotten.

DOCTOR: What is not rotten here in Denmark! That I should have to end my days in this worm-eaten, rat-ridden hyperborean keep! What revel is that below?

BOY: It is the English tragedians, who play to-night before his majesty. There, sir, I have set the stool against it. (*The murmurs from below cease.*) They present some Danish story, one framed out of matters passed here at Elsinore long ago.

DOCTOR: A dismal taste in the Lord Chamberlain Horatio. I had thought he would rather be for some bawdy tale out of Italy. How strictly does the office make the man! I knew just such another Chamberlain here, but at a time none now thinks upon.

[*The door once more blows open, this time to the accompaniment of the sound of a falling stool. The voices now following are heard clearly but as from some remove below; the stir and comment of the audience may also be perceptible.*

PLAYER HORATIO: What, has this thing appeared again to-night?

BARNARDO: I have seen nothing.

MARCELLUS: Horatio says 'tis but our fantasy,
And will not let belief take hold of him
Touching this dreaded thing twice seen of us,

20

Therefore I have entreated him along
With us to watch the minutes of this night,
That if again this apparition come,
He may approve our eyes and speak to it.

P. HORATIO: Tush, tush, 'twill not appear.

BARNARDO:                 Sit down awhile,
And let us once again assail your ears,
That are so fortified against our story,
What we have two nights seen.

P. HORATIO:                 Well, sit we down,
And let us hear Barnardo speak of this.

BARNARDO: Last night of all,
When yon same star that's westward from the pole
Had made his course t'illume that part of heaven
Where now it burns, Marcellus and myself,
The bell then beating one——

MARCELLUS: Peace, break thee off, look where it comes
    again!

BARNARDO: In the same figure like the king that's
    dead.

MARCELLUS: Thou art a scholar, speak to it, Horatio.

BARNARDO: Looks a' not like the king? mark it, Horatio.

P. HORATIO: Most like, it harrows me with fear and
    wonder.

BARNARDO: It would be spoke to.

MARCELLUS: Question it, Horatio.

P. HORATIO: What art thou that usurp'st this time of
night,
Together with that fair and warlike form
In which the majesty of buried Denmark
Did sometimes march? by heaven I charge thee speak.

MARCELLUS: It is offended.

BARNARDO: See, it stalks away.

P. HORATIO: Stay, speak, speak, I charge thee speak.

DOCTOR (*testily*): Shut the door; shut it, I say! These are
but ragged fellows strutting and mouthing it through
some old wives' tale. (*The* BOY *again secures the door*.)
The smoke from this pestilent garret fire is in my eyes.
Read on, boy, in good Doctor Bright.

BOY (*reads*): "Melancholy breedeth a ielousie of doubt,
and causing them to be the more exact and curious in
pondering, destroyeth the braine with all his faculties
and disposition of action."

DOCTOR: How the wind whispers like a summons round
these battlements to-night! It seems to call my mind
back to some forgotten struggle. And the sea—do you
hear it calling too?

BOY: Calling, sir?

DOCTOR: Aye—or to a melancholy man I say it would
call. Can you not hear what it might say to such a
one?

22

Listen: now . . . and now . . . and now.

[*Each repetition of the word "now" has been timed by the*
  DOCTOR *to coincide with the deep reverberation of a wave*
  *below.*

BOY: Sir, the tide is at the full, and I hear only the
waves that break in the deep cavities of the cliff. . . .
Shall I read further? (*Reads*) "The house seemeth vnto
the melancholicke person a prison or dungeon——"

DOCTOR: Denmark's a prison.

BOY: Sir?

DOCTOR: Nay, how the ventricle of memory begins to
open at that word! Tell me, boy, what is the argument
of this Danish tragedy that these English players
give?

BOY: One that many doubted his majesty's liking of. It
is the story of Prince Hamlet, old King Hamlet's son,
who killed his uncle, Claudius, upon some occasion
never, men say, fully ravelled out.

DOCTOR: Even so it was. I have some occasion to
remember the prince—the poor melancholic prince! He
would have figured with good concernancy in Master
Bright's treatise. But these travelling players, gibbering
before some filthy sheeted ghost, peddle mere eggs in
moonshine. Yet open the door, boy, and for some
moments let us hear these shadows.

BOY (*aside*): Old Mungobungo hear a play—truly
wonders pass not from the earth!

DOCTOR (*while the* BOY *crosses the chamber and moves away the stool*): Aye, that prince would have figured aptly in Master Bright's treatise. I marked such a place but now. (*Turns pages and reads*) "The mind fancieth not according to truth; but, as the nature of that humour leadeth it, altogether gastely and fearfull. Fantasie forgeth disguised shapes, which give great terror unto the heart . . ."

[*The* BOY *pulls the door open and the* PLAYERS' *voices are again heard.*

P. HORATIO:  Look, my lord, it comes!

PLAYER HAMLET: Angels and ministers of grace defend us!
Be thou a spirit of health, or goblin damned,
Bring with thee airs from heaven, or blasts from hell,
Be thy intents wicked, or charitable,
Thou com'st in such a questionable shape,
That I will speak to thee. I'll call thee Hamlet,
King, father, royal Dane. O, answer me!
Let me not burst in ignorance, but tell
Why thy canonized bones hearsed in death
Have burst their cerements? why the sepulchre,
Wherein we saw thee quietly inurned,
Hath oped his ponderous and marble jaws
To cast thee up again? what may this mean
That thou, dead corse, again in complete steel
Revisits thus the glimpses of the moon,
Making night hideous, and we fools of nature
So horridly to shake our disposition
With thoughts beyond the reaches of our souls?
Say why is this, wherefore? what should we do?

P. HORATIO: It beckons you to go away with it,
As if it some impartment did desire
To you alone.

24

MARCELLUS:          Look with what courteous action
It waves you to a more removed ground,
But do not go with it.

P. HORATIO:          No, by no means.

P. HAMLET: It will not speak, then I will follow it.

P. HORATIO: Do not, my lord.

P. HAMLET:          Why, what should be the fear?
I do not set my life at a pin's fee,
And for my soul, what can it do to that
Being a thing immortal as itself;
It waves me forth again, I'll follow it.

P. HORATIO: What if it tempt you toward the flood, my
    lord,
Or to the dreadful summit of the cliff
That beetles o'er his base into the sea,
And there assume some other horrible form,
Which might deprive your sovereignty of reason,
And draw you into madness? think of it—
The very place puts toys of desperation,
Without more motive, into every brain
That looks so many fathoms to the sea
And hears it roar beneath.

[*The murmur of the audience is brought up, and* KING
    FORTINBRAS *and* HORATIO *are heard whispering.*

FORTINBRAS: Why, Horatio, the players deal not ill with
you in those closed-up years. A pretty speech!

HORATIO: Aye, very good, very good. I had something
that trick of it indeed. It may be that later they will
something touch your majesty too.

P. HAMLET:              It waves me still.
Go on, I'll follow thee.

P. HORATIO: You shall not go, my lord.

P. HAMLET:              Hold off your hands.

P. HORATIO: Be ruled, you shall not go.

P. HAMLET:              My fate cries out,
And makes each petty artere in this body
As hardy as the Nemean lion's nerve;
Still am I called, unhand me, gentlemen,

*[Sound of struggle, and of a sword drawn.*

By heaven I'll make a ghost of him that lets me!
I say, away! go on, I'll follow thee.

BOY: Sir, sir, may I go down; oh, may I? *I* do not think
is it like shadows that these players speak, nor that their
tale is eggs in moonshine. And could this prince indeed
be such a one as Master Bright discourses of—the
melancholic man ever curiously considering amid
doubt and diffidence, without disposition to action? To
me he sounds rather as a man of fiery spirit, swift in
stratagem and minded to heroic deeds.

DOCTOR: Nay, shut the door, and this time set the great
chest against it. With what pernicious force do these
players conjure up what was not, nor can be! They are
nought—do you hear me?—I say nought! So long as
they set idle and dinner-surfeited spectators a-gape for

an hour, they care not whether their creations be in or out of Nature's family. What reck they of the judicious censure of men well-seen in the coherence and inter-dependency of human passions; men even such as Timothy Bright indeed, boy, explorers both laborious and subtle of the very *arcana* of the mind? I do recall that young Prince Hamlet well. His disorder lay open to me, and from each stage of it could I, his physician, prognosticate the next. But i'faith what a sad change will he have suffered at these tragedians' hands, the mark and acme of whose ambition is but a gallimaufry of emotions, a fantastical herd of incompatible humours yoked violently together, the better to bump and jolt the crazy waggon of Thespis up hill and down dale, through bush, through briar: mere *furor poeticus*, huff-snuff, and rim-raff-rum!

BOY (*aside*): Beastly Mungobungo! Silly old fool!

DOCTOR: Say you, say you?

BOY: The stool, sir. I will set it here by the taper's light and read on. (*Aside*) Now Morpheus and Master Bright's most drowsy cadences aid me! (*Reads*) "Neither only is common sense and fantasie ouertaken with delusion, but memory also receiveth a wound therewith: which disableth it both to keep in memory . . ."

[*The* BOY's *voice grows fainter and is lost in the sound of the wind and the waves. Presently the* DOCTOR *is heard snoring.*

BOY: Praise be to Saint Nicholas, who knows what is best for young boys and old scholars! Now pray that I be not too late for some gory close. Away with the chest,

27

and take this taper, and down Mungobungo's winding stair—may he break his neck on it yet! Now!

[*As the* Boy *opens the door there is heard—prolonged and realistic—the death-rattle of* King Claudius.

Oh, joy! They're dying! Sleep soundly, Mungobungo!

[*What follows comes faintly at first and then in increasing volume as the* Boy *descends the staircase.*

Laertes:                    He is justly served,
It is a poison tempered by himself.
Exchange forgiveness with me, noble Hamlet,
Mine and my father's death come not upon thee,
Nor thine on me!

P. Hamlet: Heaven make thee free of it! I follow thee.

[Hamlet *is heard to fall heavily, both the rapier and the cup which he has just directed against* Claudius *clattering to the ground beside him.*

I am dead, Horatio. Wretched queen, adieu!
You that look pale and tremble at this chance,
That are but mutes or audience to this act,
Had I but time, as this fell sergeant, Death,
Is strict in his arrest, O, I could tell you——
But let it be; Horatio, I am dead,
Thou livest, report me and my cause aright
To the unsatisfied.

P. Horatio:            Never believe it;
I am more an antique Roman than a Dane——

[*At this there is a sound of subdued laughter from the audience.*

Here's yet some liquor left.

P. HAMLET:                    As thou'rt a man,
Give me the cup, let go, by heaven I'll have it!

[*It is at this line that the play is heard at full volume, the* BOY
*having entered the hall. Sounds of struggle, panting, the
cup dashed to the ground.*

O God, Horatio, what a wounded name,
Things standing thus unknown, shall live behind me!
If thou dids't ever hold me in thy heart,
Absent thee from felicity awhile,
And in this harsh world draw thy breath in pain,
To hear my story——

[*During this speech the tramp of an army has made itself heard
advancing; at* HAMLET's *last word it stops, there is a
sound as of grounded arms, and this is followed by a loud
detonation.*

What warlike noise is this?

OSRIC: Young Fortinbras, with conquest come from
  Poland,
To th'ambassadors of England gives
This warlike volley.

[*At the name "Fortinbras" the audience breaks into applause,
which drowns the reference to the ambassadors.* HORATIO
*and* KING FORTINBRAS *are again heard in whispered
comment.*

HORATIO: So, so! Now we come to it! Let your majesty
be prepared to take gracious notice of the general
acclamation.

FORTINBRAS: I see, my fox, that you would put this
tragedy to some strange employment.

29

P. HAMLET:     O, I die, Horatio,
The potent poison quite o'er-crows my spirit,
I cannot live to hear the news from England,
But I do prophesy th'election lights
On Fortinbras

[*Loud applause.*

————he has my dying voice.
So tell him, with th'occurrents more and less
Which have solicited—the rest is silence.

P. HORATIO: Now cracks a noble heart. Good night,
    sweet prince!
And flights of angels sing thee to thy rest!

[*An immediate and loud roll of kettle-drums.*

Why does the drum come hither?

HORATIO (*agitated whisper*): Mark, now, mark! Aye, the
music screws them up to it bravely. Be ready, your
majesty. Here he comes, the very shadow of your
youth!

[*Marching steps, a halt called by the drums, and a General
    Salute, or music of like military consequence.*

PLAYER FORTINBRAS: Where is this sight?

[*The audience breaks into loud and prolonged applause, punctu-
    ated by cries of "Long live the King!" and "God save
    King Fortinbras!" The noise of Music breaks into the
    Danish National Anthem, which the audience rises and
    sings. At the end of this there is renewed applause, from
    amid which* KING FORTINBRAS *is heard to speak.*

FORTINBRAS: I thank you, my lords . . .

HORATIO: Silence!

FORTINBRAS: I thank you, my lords, I thank you, good people all, for this most grateful show of loyalty. But now I beg you to resume your seats and allow these worthy players to proceed.

[*The audience is heard to sit down again.*

HORATIO (*clapping his hands*): Proceed, mummers, proceed!

P. FORTINBRAS: Where is this sight?

P. HORATIO: What is it you would see?
If aught of woe or wonder, cease your search.

P. FORTINBRAS: This quarry cries on havoc. O proud death,
What feast is toward in thine eternal cell,
That thou so many princes at a shot
So bloodily hast struck?

P. HORATIO:                    Give order that these bodies
High on a stage be placed to the view,
And let me speak to th'yet unknowing world
How these things came about; so shall you hear
Of carnal, bloody and unnatural acts,
Of accidental judgements, casual slaughters,
Of deaths put on by cunning and forced cause,
And, in this upshot, purposes mistook
Fall'n on th'inventors' heads: all this can I
Truly deliver.

P. FORTINBRAS:                    Let us haste to hear it,
And call the noblest to the audience.
For me, with sorrow I embrace my fortune,
I have some rights of memory in this kingdom

[*Applause.*

Which now to claim my vantage doth invite me . . .

[*The applause and loyal acclamations of the audience now drown
    the play. But* KING FORTINBRAS *and* HORATIO *can be
    heard whispering.*

HORATIO: Hark at them, your majesty! Now, this will be
talked of throughout Denmark!

FORTINBRAS: My excellent Chamberlain a nicely man-
aged scene, indeed. The players can make no head
against it.

HORATIO: What?

FORTINBRAS: I say, the players can make no head against
it. Sign to them to have done.

HORATIO: Conclude, mummers!

P. FORTINBRAS (*bellowing*): Take up the bodies; such a
    sight as this
Becomes the field, but here shows much amiss.
Go, bid the soldiers shoot.

[*A Dead March, and ordnance shot off amid the continuing
    applause and general chatter of the audience.*

FORTINBRAS: My lords, we thank you. . . . Nay, sirs, we
are beholden to you all. . . . Good night, then, heartily.

... My lord—and you, my lord. ... Nay, my dear lady, we thank you for thus gracing us. ...

HORATIO: Aye, sir, indeed, his majesty is in high pleasure. ... Good night, my lord. ... You, sirrah, see that these players have entertainment. ... Wine? You may go so far, you may go so far—but, mark, not to drunkenness! ... Your ladyship's servant, your ladyship's servant. ... Good night. Good night!

[*The courtiers take their leave and the hum of voices dies away.*

Your majesty is not offended by this fetch of mine?

FORTINBRAS: Horatio, it was a masterpiece of the statist's skill! Did you mark how the envoys of our covetous neighbour glowered when the court cheered the bold claim of that player-king, that other I, to the crown of Denmark? How was it? "I have some rights of memory in this kingdom, Which I embrace——"

HORATIO: Nay, your majesty, it went not so. "Which now to claim my vantage doth invite me." I'faith, 'twas well; 'twas very well. Would Plato, think you, have cast out these pestilent poets from his commonwealth, had he with the like subtlety considered the uses of them? Aye, marry, it came to me like an inspiration, like a very divine *enthousiasmos*. There stood these same players in the base-court in a nipping winter air, the chief of them with his schedule of revels—comedies, tragedies, pastorals or what you will—and in the midst, *Hamlet Prince of Denmark*! On the instant I set my finger to it, so. "That plays's the thing," I said. "The ship of state sails thus, and there is needful (or rather there is to be desired, or to be hoped—for straitly needful 'tis not) some breath—but free and unconjured, mark!—of

the affection that the better sort in Denmark do bear
King Fortinbras. And for that yon play's the thing!"

FORTINBRAS: It answered well. But see, the hall is
voided, and we will have a posset brought to us by
yonder fire, which still holds warmth enough to yield
some comfort to old limbs. Where is my page? You, boy!
carry the lord Horatio's stool, and kneel then by the fire
and ply those bellows. So, 'tis very well. Did we indeed
speak with such eloquence, think you, then in our prime,
drowning the drums and trumpets and cannon with more
plangent words? Or has this English poet's feigning
turned our iron into gold?

HORATIO: Your majesty has always been noted for a
most approved and moving eloquence upon public
occasions.

FORTINBRAS: Nay, man, save such speeches for your own
public use. Never more than a blunt soldier, I. It was
young Hamlet who was a very lord of words, and so the
poet has justly represented him. Yet the poet's Horatio
had some pretty rhetoric too. (*Histrionic*) "I am more an
antique Roman than a Dane." Did you mark how some
of the younger sort behind us would fain have mocked
thee upon that? Impertinent fry! They were saying: "So
spake Horatio some forty summers past, but regard him
now, a greybeard, sitting in great place and slippered
ease." (*Laughing.*) "Here's yet some liquor left!" (*laughing again.*)

HORATION (*offended*): Your majesty forgets that the charge
laid upon me by Prince Hamlet made survival a sacred
duty. And it is so still, since my chronicle is yet far
from its term. The letters impede me much.

34

FORTINBRAS: The letters, Horatio? There are to be letters?

HORATIO: Aye, marry! Whatever be the smart new fashion, a Life, to my thinking, is no Life at all, unless it have Letters to boot. The time at Wittenberg is the rub. The prince was exchanging letters with young men all over Christendom! And the matter—when I can sound it, which is not always so—comes often a pitch too near to wild opinion—or flat heresy! So I must go carefully, by the mass. And then there be points of state, too, that ask some care—as instance the prince's mother, the late Queen Gertrude. Remember who *her* family were, and think where we should be in this awkward matter of the new timber trade if we offended *them*. These and other like weighty reasons would make publication now most inexpedient.

FORTINBRAS: It is to be seen you nurse a work of weight, and one scorning such loud appeal as these players have given their story. I but hope that yours will catch men's suffrage with an equal favour.

HORATIO (*stiffly*): My history has already been handsomely subscribed for by the nobility. And it will be a plain, unvarnished tale, a solid and well-documented work, free from fancy——

FORTINBRAS: And without a ghost?

HORATIO: Your majesty?

FORTINBRAS: The players' story has a ghost in it; nay, is a ghost story. Well, what of your Life in that?

HORATIO: Hem! As for that . . . um——

BOY: The bellows has kindled a blaze, your majesty. Shall I put another log on the fire?

FORTINBRAS: Do so, boy—and think that you may be Lord Chamberlain of Denmark one day, being so awake to relieve the embarrassments of the powerful. But come, Horatio, face it! Forty years, man, forty years since—how have these players clothed it? "Absent thee from felicity awhile, And in this harsh world draw thy breath in pain, To tell my story." But, old friend, *what* story? Volume the first: a clever student writing letters to other such. Well enough! But after that? A ghost story, or not a ghost story? How died King Hamlet in his orchard—can you tell me that? That smooth-tongued, politic, shabby rascal Claudius, that wived with the queen in so indecent a sort: had he truly poured poison in his brother's ear? Or was it rather into *young* Hamlet's ear that poison had been poured, by man or devil? Then recall the girl—how named they her?

HORATIO: Ophelia, majesty—old Polonius' daughter.

FORTINBRAS: Did the prince love her?

HORATIO: He did, and that in honest sort. There I have letters that make me most assured on't.

FORTINBRAS: Then how came he to treat her so scurvily? What manner of man was he? Confess, Horatio, that there the enigma lies, upon the very threshold of your design. Often, as you have pieced me the story together, I have thought that it is of a very Janus-figure that you

36

spoke. Recall that night upon the platform when you and your companions struggled with Hamlet, and he burst from your arms to follow some shape of terror along those crazy battlements in the dark——

HORATIO (*ringing voice*): I never loved man more in my long life than in that moment.

FORTINBRAS: There speaks the past! Recall, too, the swift design he hinted of some subtle policy of madness. Recall his cast against the usurper's creatures on the voyage to England—sudden in conception, and its execution following like the thunder the lightning's flash. Recall the impetuous sort in which his valour declared itself against the pirates, or the power with which at the last his dying hand struck that fatal cup from yours that would receive it. Aye, look on those pictures—and now on these! A brooder in corners, holding tedious argument with his own shadow. A seeker of tenuous occasions for procrastinating his own designs. One turning from the very thirst and raving of revenge to slake himself upon players' gossip and the jesting of clowns in a grave-yard! Were there two Hamlets: dreamer and doer, doubter and fanatic, pattern of courtesy and babbler of foul jests in maidens' laps? Aye—and then his end! What deepening dejection, and how nourished; what abnegation of all care or craft, led the falcon blind into a springe the very mole had eyed and turned from? . . . Horatio, was this subject of your life's work sane? Or was he mad?

HORATIO: He was something of a philosopher and something of a poet—betwixt-and-between sorts both, where madness stands in question. I find the doctors of Wittenberg spoke most highly of him; an ominous augury, your majesty will agree, in any heir apparent. He thought too much, and so ever fell into some posture of helplessness, dropping his shield to scan its other side. You and I well know how in statecraft there breathes no leisure for circumspection of *that* kind.

FORTINBRAS: You judge him one in whom the power of action was ever hard to win, a student ill sorted with a task of blood. Yet I see him not as being in nature such a man, a weakling upon whom the burdens incident to his rank and order in our strenuous age pressed like a more than Atlas' load. To me, he was strong.

HORATIO: It is no light or easy matter—heaven be praised!—to kill a king. And had he run Claudius through outright, with what evidence should he have satisfied the people? Your majesty has named it: a ghost story, nothing more.

FORTINBRAS: That cock will not fight, Horatio. Remember Polonius' son, Laertes, and how at a call to avenge *his* father's death the people followed him with clamour to Claudius' very audience chamber. Think you that, where Laertes succeeded, young Hamlet, the people's paragon, would have failed? I say that he was neither of a disposition too gentle for any necessary deed of violence nor yet restrained by politic consideration or physical impediment from killing Claudius like a rat.

BOY: My master says that rats must be hard to kill at Elsinore. He says that the castle swarms with them and that they breed diseases.

HORATIO: Small boys should be seen and not heard—the more particularly in the royal presence.

FORTINBRAS: Yet there is something in what the lad's master says, whoever he may be. Look into it, Horatio. Where did I lately hear of one had some success with rats? In Hamlin, I believe it was. Look to it. But for the matter. I say that the young prince had means and strength and purpose too, but that there lurked in the metal of that purpose some flaw that broke the blade. Or change the figure, Horatio, and say that under whatever mine was laid by Hamlet for blowing Claudius skyhigh there dug some deeper pioneer, and that in the issue the workings gave and crumbled to such general ruin as these English players showed. Now, who was that counter-ingener?

HORATIO: Perhaps some man of moral scruple, a confessor or other holy person.

FORTINBRAS: Scruples bred so, a man would discuss with his familiar friend, yet have you never talked, Horatio, of young Hamlet's speaking to you after that fashion. I scent some rarer doubt. In the beginning no more than a tendril round the trunk—as is shown by his first resolute behaviour—it grew by watering, until that most excellent mind and spirit, a tree with spread enough, Horatio, to shade a score of such common fellows as we are, was choked and killed. Whence came that watering?

BOY: My master——

HORATIO: What we know not now, we are never like to know. There be not many save ourselves in Denmark surviving from those times, and none surely whose counsel I have not sounded long ere this.

BOY: My lord, have you sounded my master?

HORATIO: Quiet, boy!

FORTINBRAS: This is no page of mine. Who are you, boy, and how came you here?

BOY: Your majesty was graciously pleased to take me by the ear as I pressed forward at the play, and bid me tend the fire. I serve the worthy Doctor Mungo.

FORTINBRAS: And your good Doctor's memory harks back to this Prince Hamlet whose story we have seen enacted?

BOY: Only to-night, your majesty, I heard my master speak of him as one whom he had physicked for a morbid melancholy.

FORTINBRAS: This passes wonder. Fetch hither your master. Horatio, who is this Mungo?

HORATIO: Some ill physician——

BOY: An't please you, my lord, old Mungobungo is a very good physician, albeit, as old men are, a nasty and most ugglesome dotard.

HORATIO: Begone, you squash, and fetch your master. And look you mock him not, nor other elderly persons deserving reverence.

BOY: I fly!

[*The* BOY *departs, whistling.*

HORATIO: Beshrew me, but I'll not believe it. Mungo! I do recall him—I do recall him! He came hither, well-reputed, out of Scotland, and had some countenance from idle women of the court when sick from love. By these and other humorous folk he came to much practice. But later, the fashion changing, he fell from favour, and now lives in I know not what corner of the castle on some small bounty from your majesty. They use him to drench horses. *He* can know nought of Hamlet.

FORTINBRAS: Then, Horatio, shall he and I start square, however it may be with the official historiographer.

[*The* BOY's *whistling is heard again in growing volume.*]

BOY: Just in time, your majesty. The rats had almost made a meal of the good Doctor. See where he comes.

[*Shuffling footsteps, the tapping of a stick, and a disturbed breathing herald the* DOCTOR's *entry into the presence.*]

DOCTOR: Your majesty's most devoted subject—and physician. It pains me to find your majesty unwell. I fear that our adventurous Doctor Lopez, and our innovating Doctor Martino——

HORATIO: Nay, man, they are skilled enough, and it is not your nostrums that the king——

FORTINBRAS: Doctor Mungo, we are glad to see that you, at least, the years are treating kindly. And it is not upon any professional occasion that we have thought to disturb a retirement so honourably earned as yours. The Lord Chamberlain and ourselves are fallen into some pleasant discourse of old times, and we would gladly have another veteran join us. Boy, set a stool for your master; aye, and a cup too. So. The matter of our talk is Hamlet, that unhappy prince whose story these English players have re-lived to-night. Do you remember him?

DOCTOR: Hamlet, did your majesty say—Prince Hamlet? No, I never knew him.

BOY (aside): Treacherous Mungobungo!

FORTINBRAS: Come, Doctor, old memories are like old badgers—hard to lure to the light. I think you knew Prince Hamlet.

DOCTOR: My art teaches that the mind gives politic burial to memories that have danger in them. He of whom you speak moved amid great affairs which such lowly men as I can have no safe concernment with.

HORATIO: Sound doctrine, by the mass, sound doctrine!

FORTINBRAS: Nay, man, there is no hazard to you. Mark how the players have rehearsed Hamlet's story for us with all the freedom of a most heightened fancy.

DOCTOR: Aye, fancy enough, I'll be bound—as if the poor young man himself had not a superplus of it.

FORTINBRAS: Aha, so now we come to it! Horatio, if the players gain a purse for their mere feigning of Hamlet's story, what must not this good Doctor have for such truth in the matter as is warranted us by his well-approved and piercing skill? Yea, and his boy too shall have somewhat—our free pardon for naming us ugglesome dotards. Truth, boy, should be greatly prized, and therefore the oftener husbanded. Doctor, proceed.

DOCTOR: Your majesty, my chamber although lofty—perhaps a trifle too lofty and something on the windy side—is within sound of the waves as they roll in upon the caverns that honeycomb the rock upon which the castle stands. And sometimes as I listen I think of the darkest and farthest pools therein, and, in these pools, of the sea-anemones which, without impulsion perceptible to us, now open to marvellous intricacy of form and colour, and now close, inert and obdurate. Such is man's memory. This very evening, listening to the wind in the battlements, my mind so stirred and opened. It was upon those battlements, and on such a night, that I came first upon the lord Hamlet, knowing not then that it was he.

HORATIO: You knew not the prince, man! How was that?

DOCTOR: I had come but lately to Elsinore, and knew little of its people—no more than that there was some dark trouble in the state. King Hamlet was dead and the election huddled over without right forms; Claudius his brother was on his throne—aye, and with something too much haste in his bed as well. Moreover there was talk of war, and the nights were loud as the days with warlike preparation. I was restless, vext by some intricate case on which hung my growing name. I climbed to the battlements and walked upon a platform there—a fearful place the unguarded edge of which seemed to pluck one's eye and very body to the beating surge below. (*The sound of the waves is heard.*) The wind caught at my cloak. (*Wind.*) High in air, birds unknown to me

43

were crying against the dark (*bird calls*), cheating the mind to fashion out some music from their calls. (*Hamlet music.*) From within the castle there came sounds of revel, the merriment of great lords who had feasted themselves well. The courtiers were drinking deep. But far below me in shipyards and arsenals—which, lit by great naphtha flares, showed like a very Tartarus in the night—men wrought at weapons. (*The clang of metal upon metal.*) And then hard by me I heard an answering sound, upon another scale. (*The sound of a knife whetted.*) I turned and saw a figure in deepest black, composing with the shade. He looked up, and I saw his face.

HAMLET: Stand, who are you?

DOCTOR: Sir, I am a physician—a court physician.

HAMLET: Then must you be a very Hercules among physicians. Where lies your practice? Can you cure vice or lance malignity?

DOCTOR: Since I am a court physician, the treatment of lunacy is of necessity my special art. I am but lately arrived here from attendance upon a sufferer in Scotland, my own country—one actually in the reigning family, my good sir! Or in the late reigning family, perhaps I ought to say.

HAMLET: Did you achieve your patient's recovery, Doctor?

DOCTOR: Unhappily the patient would not minister to herself—a most necessary co-operation. The treatment was broken off—always a *very* dangerous thing—and the end was fatal. But *that*, I charge against the distressed

44

condition of the place, one from which I judged it well to depart in something of a hurry. They called it Dunsinane. It felt like a prison.

HAMLET: Denmark is a prison, Doctor; pray heaven you have not wriggled off the spit but to stew in the tallow-catch. And this court is beyond your labours; avoid it, or I augur you will have bad dreams. You practise surgery too?

DOCTOR: Aye, sir.

HAMLET: Pray then judge of this dagger I am whetting. Will it pass smoothly, think you, between the ribs of a gross man?

DOCTOR (*with a cry of alarm*): Sir, have a care! And who are you?

HAMLET: I am one that lives obscurely pensioned here in the most religious and illustrious King Claudius' court.

DOCTOR: And you would kill a man?

HAMLET (*matter of fact*): Assuredly. (*Renewed sound of whetting.*) And that this very night.

DOCTOR: Most interesting! And, pray, what offence has your enemy done you?

HAMLET: Offence! Nay, no offence. He has but murdered my father and whored my mother, and I, a strange, fantastical fellow, am minded to revenge. Aye, to revenge.

45

DOCTOR: Heyho! You disappoint me, sir. I had thought to find something novel in this matter. But of just such a misfortune as yours have I heard from many men—to the music of rustling straw and clanking chains. Nay, look not angrily. I would but help you.

HAMLET: My occasions, Doctor, yield no leisure for this discourse. Moreover your voice in the dark is one in which I read some arrogance of doctrine. Fare you well.

DOCTOR: Ah, one of the kittle kind! Tell me but this: is he for whom you destine that dagger easy of access, or is he to be approached only by devious policy?

HAMLET: I practise such a policy. These many days past have I feigned an antic disposition, a heavy lumpish imbecility, and I am thereby thought one of no weight or observation. And thus can I spy out my chance unheeded.

DOCTOR: Are you married?

HAMLET: Aye, Doctor, I am but lately married to certain unquiet and urgent thoughts that will not let me sleep o' nights. These are bride enough for me.

DOCTOR: I judged that you might have learnt this policy, this antic disposition, of your bairns. For often children feign just so, aping one so innocent as to have no power to judge. And this they do that they may spy unheeded upon matters apt to engage their curiosity: such matters, sir, as pass between man and woman—or between a mother, maybe, and her new lover.

HAMLET: Alas, you know not my mind's eye, good doctor, or you would not cast thus wildly in the matter. There needs no spying to come at any picture of that sort—nay at a gallery of such. Fie, man, think you that, like a worn-out lecher, I must peer through the chink of ocular proof to rouse my passion to *this* deed, this single thrust of steel to the murderer's heart? I tell you, let me but close my eyes—no, not that, not even that!—and straight there haunt me, where images of sanctity should only stand, pictures more foul, more cunningly perverse or simply sinful, than any of those the Roman painter limned to match the salt luxury of Aretino's rimes. These pictures I must blot, or perish to all wholesome thought. Yes, these filthy imaginations of the act I needs must lay . . . as one would lay a ghost. (*In a flare of passion*) Great heaven, I'll have him buried prone, that the bride he covers in my fancy be but dust!

DOCTOR: Good sir, you are wrought indeed to an extreme! But tell me this. Had one man killed your father, and had another then possessed your mother, would the sum of your passion against these two match in any sort your passion against the one that has done both? Or, granted your anger were as great, would these two men's several deeds have roused the strange perturbation—the horror, shame, guilt, baffled will—that springs from the coupled deeds laid to the one man's charge?

HAMLET: I see that in these new subtleties you would put me to a dangerous school. But my cloak though inky, Doctor, is no longer cut after the scholar's fashion.

DOCTOR: Satisfy me at least in this: how acted you when you saw this wicked uncle slay your father?

HAMLET: I saw it not. It was a secret deed, worked by poison in an orchard, and it is given out that my father died of the bite of an adder.

DOCTOR: But you are wiser, and know the truth; know it perhaps by some special favour, the voice, maybe, of an angel or guardian spirit whispering to you in the night.

HAMLET: My father's spirit has appeared to me, exposing in every circumstance the loathsome deed, and summoning me to instant vengeance.

DOCTOR: That is something! Spake the spirit of the operation of this poison?

HAMLET: Yes. Poured in my father's ear as he lay asleep, it in that instant curdled the blood, and covered his whole body with a leprous crust—a horror not to think on.

DOCTOR: No, indeed! I wonder how that poison was compounded?

HAMLET: Small matter as to that, my father being dead.

DOCTOR: I think it may a little matter. I know but one poison could work so.

HAMLET: And that?

DOCTOR: Is such as lurks in no pharmacopœia, but only in the mind of a child who, hearing with terror of the power of certain venoms, fashions their working according to the scope of his fantasy. And, indeed, in all this matter it is your own childhood—perhaps your forgotten childhood—that calls to you. You need physic for the mind.

HAMLET: Such as you carry in your wallet, my purse only being opened to you? But I will open neither purse nor mind to your fingering. Think not I fail to see your drift. You would have me view this solemn conjuration as the work of a devil that had assumed my father's form—as devils, they say, may do—to lure me to a black and causeless deed.

DOCTOR: Impute not to me, sir, an imagining so vulgar. I had rather believe it was your father's spirit indeed, than such a bug to frighten babes. That a devil may assume the form of a man is a fiction more convenient than plausible—as the holy bishop Sylvanus found when men thought to have spied him in a shameful incontinency. And this I judge that you in your better mind securely know, for the scholar's fashion sits still on your discourse if not on your body. Stay! Spake this spirit of the region whence he came?

HAMLET: Indeed, indeed he did—of sulph'rous and tormenting flames wherein he fasting bathed; of that and further torments which living ears must not be burdened with.

DOCTOR: 'Tis very well. Now, name the age at which you ceased to believe that such a region is.

HAMLET: Say you?

DOCTOR: I knew it! Not since you were a child, bolting whatever nurse or chaplain spooned you, have you believed in aught of nether flames whence such a wretched traveller might come. And here we reach the truth. If this spirit came from Purgatory its road was devious—a crook'd one through your own childish mind. Aye, Ghost and poison came from there alike.

HAMLET: I wonder, most sedate and cunning Doctor, whether yourself disproves your argument? Are *you* perhaps a devil? Would you fain catch some weakness in me: the philosopher's idleness to turn on all sides the nettle must be grasped for safety? But this is folly. For, let me tell you flat, others besides myself plainly saw the Ghost. At midnight, on this platform, certain sentinels twice marked——

DOCTOR: Good sir, look!

HAMLET: Angels and—— Nay, Doctor, it is but a drift of vapour that you see. Stare not so ghastfully.

DOCTOR (*gleeful at the success of his ruse*): Yes, and such vapours commonly haunt here at midnight, to my thinking. What further?

HAMLET: Horatio, my friend of Wittenberg, summoned to view the thing, did straightway mark it was my father.

DOCTOR: Of Wittenberg! But he knew Denmark and your father well?

HAMLET (*disturbed*): He said he saw him . . . once.

DOCTOR: Alas, good sir! And was this Ghost companioned?

HAMLET: What should companion it?

DOCTOR: Marry, on one side a cock and on the other a bull. And did it tell its tale to all these sentinels, or to you alone?

HAMLET: Do you judge, man, that it would speak of such a thing before the general? I followed it far into the darkness and there, in close secrecy, it revealed to me my uncle's treachery and my mother's guilt.

DOCTOR: Now tell me, good my lord——

HAMLET: Ha!

DOCTOR: My lord, your speech betrays you as one standing in great place here in Denmark. But tell me. Since the Ghost was silent—a mere wraith in the moonlight to all save yourself——

HAMLET: Nay, Doctor, there I have you. That it had voice those sentinels will avouch. For when it had faded on my sight and they, together with Horatio, had joined me, I thought good to administer an oath to them, and on my sword I bade them swear. Now mark. Four times did my father's spirit, as from the very ground beneath our feet, repeat that word as a grave exhortation to them all, sighing "Swear."

DOCTOR: I think I hear him now.

HAMLET: Say you?

DOCTOR: And that these same ghostly sighs, unlaid and unappeased no matter what rash vengeance you accomplish, will exhale in this place until the seas are dry. Hark.

*[There is heard as before the resonant breaking of the waves in caverns below, and at each reverberation the* DOCTOR *speaks.*

DOCTOR: Swear . . . swear . . . swear.

HAMLET: No . . . *no . . . NO!*

*[Wind and waves fade to silence.*

BOY: I do not think my master should have striven to disabuse the young prince so. Were it my sanity was in question I had rather believe a wilderness of ghosts pursued me than be lured into such doubting of myself.

HORATIO: If this tale be true, here are whole chapters like to come unstitched, and I must to my inkhorn again. How judges your majesty?

FORTINBRAS: I perceive that upon young Hamlet, bent to perform his duty, stumbled our good Doctor here, bent with an equal urgency on his, and that from their encounter sprang much mischief. Had the prince been left in the enjoyment of his natural resolution, and whetted his dagger undisturbed, Claudius, whether fratricide or no, would have gone unmourned to his account with no great moil; Denmark been ruled by a youth of genius, his temper tried by a grave and dangerous act; and myself, Horatio, had grown old in my native Norway—where indeed I find my sere thoughts often to turn with longing. But since the Doctor, judging Hamlet's mind a muddied well, yet stretched his endeavour to find truth at the bottom of it, he is by no means to be condemned. Boy, fill your master's cup again, since I apprehend that wine is the element in which the sea-creature of *his* memory best unfolds itself. And now let us see what further doubts he bred. . . . Good Doctor Mungo, break the abstraction into which you have fallen. We would hear more—although I mark, indeed, that the Lord Chamberlain's head doth a little begin to nod. Proceed.

DOCTOR: I am your majesty's to command. Thus, then, did I strive to grapple with this fiction forged by the melancholic humour of the prince from drifting vapour and a sound of breaking waves. That he was shaken, I could see. Hesitation, and a prompting to inquire within himself, took issue with that brisk resolve to yerk his uncle through the ribs forthwith. And thus, at least, had I gained time.

HORATIO (*yawning*): By the mass, this holds some consonancy with the event. For Hamlet, in truth, strangely faltered many days.

DOCTOR: Time had I gained; yet that was little. For I knew well how strong are such depraved conceits as the prince was urged by, and what deep currents move them. I made a tryst to meet him there on the platform on certain following nights, further to sound his mind. Moreover, before leaving him, I drew him to a test. What I asked, could assure us that the Ghost was verily his father's spirit? Only this: that its revelation be proved true—and that its truth be such as Prince Hamlet could by no common means have come by. We could well believe that Claudius had poisoned his royal brother— when Claudius owned to it! But dead men own to nothing. And so by this shift I left the prince at least no longer prompt to instant violence, but rather plotting means whereby the usurper might be lured to betray

53

himself. And while he was thus toiled in futile practice I trusted to search out with him whatever in his past history had sown the seed of lunacy—of this lush growth from amid the which his more wholesome mind now peered but hardly out.

HORATIO: A good figure, by the mass, Doctor. "Now peered but hardly out"—a good figure, indeed!

DOCTOR: There passed some interval of time during the which I failed not of my eyes, nor of my ears either, about the court. I heard how Hamlet loved Ophelia, but of late had become first laggard in his suit and next foul in imagination, as if she nested in his thought close to forbidden matters, or memories which the tormented mind had thought well to seal away. I noted well, therefore, the likelihood of meeting again with this girl somewhere near the quick of the malady—a malady by which I would assure your majesty that I was much distressed, as who would not be by this horrid hallucination of murder done by your majesty's august predecessor, the most devout King Claudius?

FORTINBRAS: Yours, Doctor, are most proper sentiments. It is to be hoped that they did not a little cloud your professional judgement forty years ago. Proceed.

DOCTOR: Day by day dejection grew upon the prince, and I could see that soon it would be kill or cure with him. Then came the strolling players to Elsinore and he framed his mouse-trap—the trick by which he'd make his uncle own his guilt. I marked its springing, here in this very hall. The night—as you, my Lord Chamberlain, will well remember—ended in wild confusion. From cellarage to garrets King Claudius' Switzers searched for men knew not what, and in every ear spoke apprehension and strange conjecture. (*A sound as of hue and cry about the castle is brought some way forward during the remainder of the speech.*) I climbed to the battlements and soon, panting and breathless, the Lord Hamlet followed me, and there poured out a hodgepodge of sense and nonsense. I learnt he had stabbed Polonius, and knew that of his strong disease this was the very crisis, and that the knife must be set to it now or never. I must pierce and drain whatever was the hidden ulcer irked his mind, or mere madness waited him.

HAMLET (*greatly excited*): I say I'll take the Ghost's word for a thousand pound.

DOCTOR: Aye, so, my lord—and where has it led you to-night? To the rash deed, you say, of killing the lord Polonius—Ophelia's father. Is the poor girl orphaned now, or does her mother live?

VOICES OF THE GUARD (*just intelligible*): Guard the great staircase, ho! . . . My lord, come forth. . . . Let each man seek the prince. . . . Bolt up those outward doors. . . . My lord, it is the king commands your presence. . . .

HAMLET: I know not. Hark how they bay me! But I will slip them yet—yes, down the sheer outward wall, my dagger at my back, and to my uncle's chamber by a secret way.

DOCTOR (*quick interest*): You say you know not whether the king's chief councillor has a wife that lives or not?

HAMLET (*flare of anger*): I know nought of her, I say, nor ever have!

55

DOCTOR: So . . . so! Well, to your mouse-trap. You judge it caught the king, this *Murder of Gonzago* that your players played before him?

HAMLET: It did . . . it did! And thereby are all the torturing questions you have bred in me these many days now blown to Limbo! The adulterous beast, the treacherous fratricide, rose in confusion and broke up the play.

DOCTOR: In confusion? I thought it rather in anger. For I was present, my lord, and there was little that I failed to mark. First a dumb show, in which one poisoned a king in his garden and took his crown and then his queen. It fitted your Ghost's story like a glove—yet I observed not that King Claudius was troubled thereby.

HAMLET: Pah, none heeds a dumb show. It was the play itself was the thing.

DOCTOR: And that told indeed the same story. There on the stage was your poisoner pouring his poison into a sleeping man's ear. And how comported himself King Claudius then? He watched in some distaste, maybe, but I assure you without discomposure.

HAMLET: You lie, rascally apothecary! The foul lecher, the salt and bloody butcher rose——

DOCTOR: *There*, my lord, is why the king rose; you have even now exampled it. Not the representation of a poisoning made him stir; that passed and he sat silent still. But *you* were not silent. Already with a hysterical bawdry had you offended every woman within hearing . . . and especially the lady Ophelia. And now did you

56

interrupt the play to cry out against the king in plain hostility and patent frenzy. Much offended, he rose and left the hall. . . . Good my lord, I would have you cast these false imaginings away before heavier mischief happen. Have you seen the king since?

HAMLET: Yes. As I passed to my mother's closet I marked him. But—and lucky 'twas for him—he was on his knees at prayer.

DOCTOR: At prayer! The good, pious man, praying for you, my lord, in this your sad distemperature, or thanking heaven for his own blameless life. He kill a brother —madness! Aye, madness—I speak the word most solemnly. But yet are you capable of discourse of reason; exercise it, my lord, I beg . . . Hark how they seek for you hither and thither about the castle!

VOICES OF THE GUARD: Has no man yet found him? 'Sblood, man, the king rages! Hola! . . . Search you the gallery and the farther rooms. . . . Call out the morning guard. . . . Hola! My lord . . . my lord! . . . Your highness must to the king! . . .

HAMLET: He would despatch me to England—the fly, the pawing knave, the fingerer! But whither I will despatch *him*——

DOCTOR: Then is my time with you the shorter. In your father's name, outraged by these sad events, I charge you to listen, and to answer me! When read you first that old Italian story of Gonzago's murder?

HAMLET: What care I when I read it first? Enough that it has tript the leaper by the heels.

57

DOCTOR: I tell you, you must care! I say King Claudius, watching the play yon players framed from the Italian story, saw mirrored in it no such guilty action as your wildered mind had hoped for. The play's talk of hasty marriage with a dead man's wife offended him indeed——

HAMLET: And well it might offend him! A man who has lain twixt sheets that held still the very warmth and impress of a corse! Let me not see it! God, let me not see it more!

DOCTOR: I say that however the play's hasty marriage wrung him, the poisoning was a blank. And this tells us what? That Claudius murdered no brother after that fashion! But, this being so, and the Ghost's tale having here no fount or source in fact, whence came it to that same Ghost? Think! Can you believe your uncle Claudius killed his brother, being careful, the while, to follow some mouldy old Italian story as pat as a player his written speech? It is a chance too remote for credence. No, you had from the Ghost the tale you did only because this old story of Gonzago lurked deep in your own brain. And you, my lord, for certain ends beyond your ready knowledge, but which presently my art will make clear to you, cast that tale outwards upon a mere illusion yourself had summoned up from mist and the fears of idle sentinels.

HAMLET: No!

DOCTOR: My lord, my lord, no man considering with a clear mind could give other explanation hearing. But still there are two riddles we must answer before your distracted spirit may be eased. Why, your father dying

58

in his orchard, should your mind engender this horrible fantasy of murder by one of his own blood? And why should this fantasy, huddling together your father's death and an old Italian tale, catch in its toils a lady seemingly foreign to it all, forcing you to turn in loathing and an obscure horror from your love, the innocent and gentle Ophelia? . . . I think you loved your father.

HAMLET: Indeed I did.

DOCTOR: How intolerable then would be any breath of thought that once you had wished him ill! Yet love and hate weave like a tangled skein about the human heart. And every child, loving his mother—and from that so strong love comes all love of women—has on a time most passionately willed his father straight out of the picture; nay, wished for that father some vague dismissal such as seems to a child our dreaded name of death.

HAMLET: This is flat stuff and nonsense. No thought so unimaginably horrible——

DOCTOR: Aye, so . . . quite so; you run ahead of me! This thought is sin, and so the fearful mind must drive it deep to cover. Suppose, my lord, you *had* once, say in almost infancy, thus involved your father in thoughts of death. Time has no power to rase such thoughts from the mind; it merely hides them. Well, your father dies, and then those old and much condemned thoughts stir, deep in that cave of childish cogitation where they harbour still. Such stirring—the appalled sense of some irreparable evil we have done—we know as guilt——

HAMLET: Guilt! I wonder, Doctor, have you ever felt the words you finger through the thick glove of your art?

Guilt! The rank corruption that the mind must take from that on which it gazes, the dunghill kiss the very air must suffer——

DOCTOR: My lord, let be, and listen—only listen. An act which we once performed in fantasy, and with but little understanding of its true weight and meaning, we begin to bleed for as if it had been fact. . . . And this, I believe, one of your searching mind would, upon some thought, assent to.

HAMLET: You spin such a cobweb as the schoolmen do, building up what indeed holds coherency within its own several parts, but is more likely to ensnare than to salve. It touches me not.

DOCTOR: Only listen further. You have marked how children, chidden for some naughty act, will pass the matter off after this fashion: "It was not I, it was not I! 'twas he, I say; 'twas he that did it!"—pointing the while with urgent finger at some blameless playmate; or even inventing a culprit out of fantasy, a perpetual invisible scapegoat conveniently housed in some cupboard of the nursery.

HAMLET (*agitated*): No, no!

DOCTOR: Aye, you are quick, my lord—and again ahead of me! It is in just this way that the grown mind works when its own imagined guilt would rise to overwhelm it. That guilt has slumbered long, and the man knows nothing of it. But then comes some disruptive and affraying event—the death, say, of a father—and the old guilt stirs, prowling again within its cave. So out, my lord, must come that scapegoat from the cupboard—

with, can you not hear what cry? "It was not I, of all our blood, held any guilty thought against my father. Nay, by the Gods, 'twas he!" And so you fashion out your father's Ghost, an apparition framed by yourself, I say, for the comfort of your own inner mind, that points at old, bad uncle Claudius and cries: "Aye, he did it! It was he that killed my father the better to enjoy my mother's love."

HAMLET (*breathing fast*): Pah—words, words, words!

DOCTOR: And—more—it is because this cupboard-uncle of your fantasy springs from your own once-nursed desire, that you have in truth—yes, my lord, acknowledge it!—felt strangely charmed from striking at him— except indeed in words, words, words.

HAMLET: I say this touches me not. There is that within me rejects it plainly.

DOCTOR: Good, good!

HAMLET: How say you?

DOCTOR: This same plain rejection, this course of obstinate incredulity, is a thing that marches ever with such disease as yours. My diagnosis is confirmed by it.

HAMLET: Indeed, Doctor, the symptom is a convenient one, I think. And does the cure too come pat?

DOCTOR: My lord, my lord, jest not at this horrid time. The cure, alas, requires leisure and much counsel, such as this chill platform and your uncle's questing servants allow us now small chance of. . . . The death of a father is a sad and moving thing, yet each man's father dies——

HAMLET: Aye, so *he* said, and called my just mourning impious stubbornness!

DOCTOR: But they whose actions thereafter are swayed by visions, voices, and doubtful promptings from regions of the dark, are few. I judge that some circumstance attending your father's death has touched to urgent movement some old sore, some childish hour, perhaps, so painful that you have long been unable to drag it to the light. Could we find that——

HAMLET (*in further agitation*): Something too much of this. I respect your art, Doctor, and thank you heartily—aye, heartily—for the tender of it. Yet it holds no health for me, and convalescence in its care is no such fate as I wish for. Here is my dagger still. Hark at them, now! Farewell.

DOCTOR: Then tell me one last thing. Where did you leave the lady Ophelia to-night?

HAMLET: Leave her? Why, man, where else but in the orchard?

DOCTOR: Ha!

HAMLET: Hall, I would say. I left her in the hall—(*vehemently*) the hall, I tell you; where else? Nay, detain me not.

DOCTOR: Why spoke you that word? Think, my lord! Hall, you would have said, but your tongue failed in the utterance, and orchard burst from that deep cave to which we would penetrate. Why? Think, I say, think—for here is the thread at last that leads to the centre.

[*The voices of the Guard are again heard, and are now nearer, so that the words "Hamlet" and "My lord Hamlet" are loud and urgent.*

HAMLET: No, I say, no! Paugh, fie, fie, you long-nosed loon, you nuzzler, fingerer——

DOCTOR: Nay, I am not your uncle. Think!

HAMLET (*verging on hysteria*): Am I some stale anatomy, the guts haled out——

DOCTOR: Think!

HAMLET: —for gapers to peer into, holding the nostril the while? God, God——

[*The voices of the Guard approach closer still, and their shouts of "Hamlet," "Lord Hamlet" take the foreground.*

DOCTOR (*background*): Think!

[*From amid the deep voices of the Guard a girl's voice rises clearly in a long-drawn call.*

GIRL'S VOICE: Hamlet!

[*The men's voices are instantly silent and the girl's voice is heard again.*

GIRL'S VOICE: Hamlet! . . . Hamlet!

HAMLET (*heavy respiration*): God . . . God!

GIRL'S VOICE: Hamlet!

[*The girl's voice is followed by the sound of a clanging gate, light footsteps running, and a child passionately and irresistibly weeping.*

GIRL'S VOICE: Hamlet, child—what ails you? And where have you been? Have you . . . seen aught to hurt you?

[*The weeping continues for a moment and is then cross-faded into the sobs of the man* HAMLET, *who is in a state of violent emotional discharge. The voices of the Guard are again heard, but in the distance and fading.*

HAMLET: They brought Yorick, a jester in whom my childish mind took infinite delight, but I would accept no comfort from him. They gave me a book . . .

[*The sound of the child's weeping is momentarily renewed.*

GIRL'S VOICE: Here is a new book, Hamlet—and now you can read so well, dear playmate! Take it into the orchard whence you came—nay, take it into your mother's garden, rather—and read, and calm yourself. It's an exciting tale, I'll warrant, and fit to make you forget whatever bad thing troubles you. See, 'tis called *The Murder of Gonzago*.

HAMLET: Yes, that was the book. *The Murder of Gonzago*. And in it, too, there was a sleeping king.

DOCTOR (*gently*): So. Your memory has opened, and in that there lies good hope. Speak, my lord, and at last ease yourself of the burden which, all unknowing, you have carried through many weary years.

HAMLET: I loved my father, both from the natural bond and as knowing how his virtue matched his kingship. So much is certain ground. But the place where you would now have me tread is shadowy and insubstantial, a dark wood raised round me by your questioning and these calling voices of the Guard. I distrust all footing there.

DOCTOR: My lord, my lord, to pause is to go back on far more treacherous ways. Speak!

HAMLET: I cannot trust what I see, since its concinnity appears to be but with dreams—yes, with my direst dreams. Yet how urgent it is, and accompanied by what turmoil in my soul! . . . Did you hear voices in the air?

DOCTOR: I heard the Guard. But you?

HAMLET: A voice silent to my ear or thought these twenty winters—and yet the voice of one that I did love as I have loved no other being.

DOCTOR: Man, my lord, or woman?

HAMLET: A girl—older than I by some seven years, and already in her first maidenhood more beautiful than any lady of the court. She would play with me, and then would she let her finger travel through my hair. It was innocence and innocence, or so I judged.

DOCTOR: So judge the innocent often, my lord, and shoot far from the mark.

HAMLET: Indeed, indeed, 'tis true! But, judging so, I'd tire the day with seeking for her look or voice about the castle. It is not to be described. She was a goddess to me, and all women too—yea, sister, mother——

DOCTOR: Mother, my lord?

HAMLET: Aye, Doctor. For at night she and my mother would mingle in my sweetest dreams.

DOCTOR: Yes, yes . . . speak further!

HAMLET: What profit in so speaking, since from my childhood all this has been as matter sealed up in mere oblivion? Yet it is passing strange! That voice in air spoke to me from my life's very core of passion—and yet can I almost ask did that girl live, or in this forced and sudden retrospection do I but peer into some contrived illusion, some puppet-show or motion of which yourself, Doctor, are the master!

DOCTOR: I think, my lord, that the girl of whom you speak lived indeed; and lived—was it not?—to be the mother of Ophelia—Ophelia, whose supposed father you did this night slay.

HAMLET: She did. And so I come to it! One day I saw her pass quickly into my father's pleasure ground——

DOCTOR: An orchard?

HAMLET: A small apple-orchard, high enclosed. For an hour's space I could not follow, my tutor tasking me with some lesson. But then I ran. The gate, as seldom, stood unlocked. I entered, in confidence of frolic with those two people whom I held dearest in the world. Must I tell you what I found?

DOCTOR: You need set no close words to it, my lord.

66

HAMLET: They slept—she in the seeming pure grace of a sainted thing, a bead of dew on the lip; he, my father —and this it was that in my rage and terror drove me to unendurable stress—he, I say, in a strange posture of helplessness, as if at my childish mercy, his head thrown back and aslant, so that I could see what I had never seen before, the fine hairs growing from his nostril and his ear. In that moment—— But no, it may not be spoken.

DOCTOR: Speak, and the imposthume breaks at last!

HAMLET: In that moment could I have killed him whom I loved.

DOCTOR: Or so you judged. And yet, my lord, was the scene that set you so at jar but a common accident of our soiled humanity.

HAMLET: Call it what you will. I ran from the orchard in tempestuous grief and would by no means speak or be comforted. And then the girl, awakened and following in some shame, gave me to distract my mind the book I have marked—that same *Murder of Gonzago* that tells of a king killed in his orchard—aye, killed—because of some love borne to a woman. . . . And then my memory clouds.

DOCTOR: I think, perhaps, some distemper overtook you? And that, when that had passed, much memory had passed too?

HAMLET: 'Twas so! For many days thereafter I lay in a fever, which indeed burnt out all memory of the time. Only I know that, shortly after, the king my father ordained the marriage of my late playfellow, tender as

67

were her years, to a grave noble of the court, Polonius —one so sunk in politic matters as to have small eye to private.

DOCTOR: And small thought, maybe, for the month of a child's birth?

HAMLET: No doubt, no doubt. Alas, Ophelia! . . . This is my sunken memory—false or true.

DOCTOR: And so, my lord, all is clear at last.

HAMLET: Clear! You mock me, man. Say rather all is cast in mere confusion, and my intents melt in the acid of your conjuring.

DOCTOR: Perpend! The sudden revelation that your father stood carnally possessed of her who summed for you all that was dear in woman: did not this breed in you an impulse of hatred and destruction towards him? Have you not owned it?

HAMLET: It is a truth—if these uprising memories be true.

DOCTOR: 'Tis well! Next, this dark impulse was quickly fanned to violent fantasy by a book which, conned in a hectic hour, by a fatal chance did closely touch the matter. This too, upon condition, you grant so?

HAMLET: I do so grant it.

DOCTOR: Think, then, how the fire of that same fantasy, banked and masked, not quenched, glowed ready to let loose the flame of guilt at a touch to the coal. When came that touch?

HAMLET: Nay, man, *you* are schooling *me*.

DOCTOR: When came that touch?

HAMLET: I know well what you would have me say. It came when, in his orchard where he was wont to sleep . . . an adder ended my royal father's life. . . . An adder, not my uncle.

DOCTOR: Praise heaven, my lord, your understanding takes the leap! And, indeed, we now have, in sum, as clear a picture as my art ever gained in case of a like scope and gravity. Mark! The Ghost and its false pointing, whereby you would disclaim your supposed guilt, born like old Adam's in an orchard—eeh? Why, my lord, there's laughter there. But, then, Ophelia—alas yes, poor lady!—and your turning from her upon some waking sense of a kinship there needs no further words on. She takes it hard, my lord, and will, I think, have need of my good practice soon. But now we must consult. The time calls haste. I think I had better myself hie with all this to the good king, so careful for you, and so sorely grieved by your late sad transformation. . . . (*Alarmed*) My lord, what would you?

HAMLET: But show you that I have my dagger still, and that it stands between you and your proposal! For all this would be thought on, sir. And, first, what has this powerful art of yours achieved? It has called up yet further questionable shapes—ghosts that, nigh palpable to my seeming now, may yet fade at cock-crow, even as that other did. My father's spirit methought appeared to me from purgatorial fires. Such visitings, if our sceptic age can take them, Doctor, make reasonable sense, stand with an ordered cosmos, allow Divinity still His finger at our shaping. But the shades that you have

69

summoned come from a different place of pain, from the stricken mind of a child whose agony, suffered without desert, now deviously fathers my every seeming act of mature will. Are then our grown hopes and fears, our stretchings a little to pinch out the devil, act the man, love the saint—are these, I say, disguised effusions from some blind, infantile source? Is not this, now, a preposterous show of things, that the man should be dancing ever to the unlicked lad's forgotten tune; the lad be commanded still by the puking babe; the babe, belike, be bound by accidents beyond the portals of the womb? Does no man aim, in truth, where he fancies that his reason points the bolt? This, narrowly scanned, oppugns all order and degree; it whips the lid off Chaos! But let me say this, only this. I spy a choice, Doctor, a grave choice. For, grant sin and grace, repentance, a celestial frame where good and evil stand outside ourselves, and confess, where does the likelier proposition lie? Surely in my own unaided reading of this dark book of my father's death! But incline the other way, and sum our intellectual being as stuff but part-hewn from animal cognizance, and then *you* have it with your cunning gloss! . . . I say this must be thought on. Am I a soul upon whom one clear duty has been imposed—and that with the divine allowance surely needful to let my father's spirit walk? Or am I one indeed whose un-breeched past wished a dear parent dead; and am I therefore punished with a sore distraction, near to lunacy? No, no—here is no issue to pass on at the jump. . . . Hola, Guard, ho!

Doctor: My lord, what purpose you?

Hamlet: I am for England, Doctor, as they plan. It may be the salt breath of ocean will blow from my bewildered brain one mist or the other, my Ghost or your sunk memories. It may be that in some casual need for action —and I know not their drift of policy or how it may require quick counter—I'll find relief from these distractions which you have wrought me to. Hola, Guard, I say! But on all this, Doctor, I pledge you I will think. Aye, I'll think precisely on this night's event! Meanwhile, I thank you, sir, and leave you this (*the sound of a bag of coin set down*) as token of my good regard. Nay, sir, it is I thank you. . . . Hola, Guard: here am I—Hamlet the Dane!

[*The wind and the waves are again heard, and then, as they grow faint, a quiet regular breathing.*

BOY: Shall I wake the lord Horatio, your majesty? How cold it is! Our fire is out.

HORATIO: Out . . . out, said you? Aye, that was it. "Now peers but hardly out"—a right good figure. I must make a note of it.

FORTINBRAS: I do see, Horatio, that the good Doctor has not told his tale in vain, since it is to lend so nice a turn to some emphatic sentence. But, Doctor, is this all your tale?

DOCTOR: It is, your majesty. The young prince indeed departing for England, and the court being without apprehension of his so speedy return, I betook myself to a patient in the country, and ere I was at Elsinore again, the prince's hallucination had come to its disastrous term.

FORTINBRAS: So that your treatment unhappily availed nothing in the end?

71

Boy (*without mockery*): That thrust's unfair—you must not blame my master so. Your majesty has seen how the treatment had to be broken off. And that is always a *very* dangerous thing.

Fortinbras: I'll warrant it—and the entering on it, too. Doctor Mungo, in the long years between that night and this—when sleepless, perhaps, or in some discouragement over a distemper that mocked your highest skill—have you ever looked back and questioned?

Doctor: Your majesty must forgive me. I do not well conceive your majesty.

Fortinbras: You found Prince Hamlet in dejection and some doubt indeed, as touching his mother's indecent and perhaps criminal marriage, but yet whetting a dagger with good heart to use it. You left him, not with one more doubt, but rather with a whole crop of doubts, as novel as deep, growing between him and any issue in action. For Hamlet, who had such reach of mind, were those doubts you sowed not somewhat larger than any concerning the mere matter—grave though that was—of old King Hamlet's end? Had you not opened to him, perhaps, the vision of a climate too chill for the tree of the knowledge of good and evil to grow and bear in? And did his last dejection come from this: that you had shown him reason as having no reach beyond the moon, but as a dweller wholly amid things corruptible?

Doctor: I perceive that your majesty is not well seized of this matter, and that there stand indeed in your own mind certain impediments to a clear understanding that would be well away. May I ask if your majesty is with any frequency graciously pleased to dream?

FORTINBRAS (*hastily*): No, no, good Doctor, my dreams shall be my own, and any ghosts that haunt me private to myself. We thank you and excuse you. Now, good night.

DOCTOR: I am your majesty's devoted subject and—may I remind you?—most careful physician upon any issue.

[*The tap of the* DOCTOR'S *stick is heard as he withdraws from the royal presence; its tempo changes as he begins to climb the winding stair, and at the same time he falls to muttering.*

DOCTOR: Barbarians . . . freebooters and pirates . . . that I should have to end my days in the most comfortless corner of a brigand's den!

BOY: Nay, master, be more cheerful. Did not the king—although he may have understood you not—speak of a purse? I judge that you shall have some profit of this night's work.

DOCTOR (*with a snarl*): Profit? Profit! I tell you, boy, were I from Elsinore away and clear, *profit* again should hardly draw me here!

[*The sound of the wind and the waves has been growing as they climb, and the deep reverberation of the breakers is heard at the Close.*

# THE MYSTERIOUS AFFAIR AT ELSINORE

*A New Investigation*

*by* MICHAEL INNES

First broadcast on Sunday, June 26th, 1949

# THE MYSTERIOUS AFFAIR AT ELSINORE

## I

EVERYBODY KNOWS THAT the Elsinore affair remains unsolved. And the chances of any striking success must now seem slender. It is difficult not to suspect that by this time a good many of the clues have disappeared. Where, for example, is that arras behind which the Lord Chamberlain Polonius ensconced himself? I cannot very confidently accept the proposition that it was possible to view this important exhibit in the collection of Danish art recently on show at the Victoria and Albert Museum. It seems to me more probable that what we saw there was merely a *similar* arras. And while that, of course, might have its value—it would be serviceable in a reconstruction of the crime—we cannot lean on it too hard. That, indeed, is just what Polonius himself did, with fatal consequences.

The truth is (and we may as well face it squarely) that the matter went disastrously from the start. Here we must place the blame squarely upon the shoulders of Prince Fortinbras of Norway. *Take up the bodies*, he ordered peremptorily. But, as we all know, the bodies must on no account be moved. Whenever to-day (as constantly happens) the body of a baronet with a dubious past is discovered in the library at midnight, and outside the french windows (it is astonishing how fond baronets are of french windows) lies an untrodden carpet of snow, and the ashen-faced butler is dropping his tray with all that whisky and all those glasses, and the baronet's wife is stalling off a blackmailer in her boudoir and the cousin from Australia is tampering with the concealed safe in the billiard-room: when these common incidents in the life of the English landed gentry have yet once more transacted themselves, this one golden rule is to be observed: nobody must move the body. Even when the butler, hastily recruiting himself from the unspilled brandy, falls writhing in the agonies which must follow upon the imbibing of prussic acid; even when the blackmailer has a heart-attack and tumbles deftly and compromisingly out of the boudoir window; even when the concealed safe, disclosing itself as in fact an infernal machine, blows the bad-hat cousin sky-high: even then the bodies, be they mounting up like the snowdrifts in the spreading park outside, must on no account be moved. Yet even such a complicated holocaust as this is as nothing to that which confronted the authorities at Elsinore; and it is all the more deplorable, therefore, that this reckless order should have been given, and that thereupon *four captains* should have borne Hamlet like a soldier to the stage—a heavy-footed proceeding much like that of letting a squad of local constables loose on that all-important snow.

But consider further. We can by no means be assured that of the numerous persons presently to be buried all were already dead. For example, it is known that King Claudius, after being run through by Hamlet, declared firmly that he was *but hurt*, and it is impossible to believe that Hamlet succeeded in forcing down his throat sufficient of the poisoned wine to have any very immediate effect upon one of so robust a constitution as the late King Hamlet's brother. Moreover, I am myself strongly of the opinion that Hamlet's gesture in thrusting the goblet in Claudius's teeth was substantially symbolical, not to say theatrical; and I think that this explana-

78

tion will cohere very well with our sense of the generally excitable and fanciful disposition which this young man clearly owned. It thus appears very likely that Claudius's death was lingering, and that some dying statement might well have been secured from him, if only in an agonal whisper, had not Fortinbras destroyed this possible clue also, by ordering, in so critical a moment, that *the soldiers' music and the rite of war speak loudly,* thus drowning any possible communication of this sort beneath the blended uproars of a peal of ordnance and a military band. Nor can I refrain from remarking here upon another adverse effect of this action. It might be very useful to be able to determine what kind of poison had been employed in the goblet prepared for the fencing match. Now, everybody knows about that faint odour of bitter almonds that hangs over the baronet's library and may well have hung revealingly over the hall of the castle at Elsinore. But whether it in fact did so or not we shall never know, since the stench of gunpowder occasioned by the salvoes which Fortinbras caused to be fired off would have made any such faint fume undetectable.

## II

But I come now to what is, after all, the grand disappointment we must face in endeavouring at this late date to solve the mystery. There was one witness—one active participant, indeed—from whom much might have been expected. Let me remind you of the words in which Horatio is reported to have replied to the assertions of the soldier Marcellus on the subject of certain paranormal phenomena traditionally associated with Christmas. *So have I heard,* Horatio said, *and do in part believe it.* Nothing could better illustrate, we may feel,

79

the temperament of the born detective. To believe a little of everything you hear, and to disbelieve the rest: this is the royal road in successful criminal investigation.

We might, then, have high hopes of Horatio on this score alone, and it is surely with justified excitement that we learn a further fact. This clear-headed young man was commissioned by Hamlet himself to inquire into the whole affair and make a report to the crowner at the inquest. For I take it that, in the command *report me and my cause aright to the unsatisfied,* the words *crowner and his jury* were either actually added by the dying Hamlet and have been lost from the report, or were trembling upon his lips when he was prevented from delivering them by that rash action of Horatio's in making a grab at the poisoned cup. Be this as it may, here we have Horatio commissioned to clear up the mystery. And he was confident that he could do it; indeed, that he had all the threads already in his hands! For he proposed, you will remember, to explain, unequivocally and almost immediately, *how those things came about.* His hearers, he said, would learn

> Of carnal, bloody and unnatural acts,
> Of accidental judgements, casual slaughters,
> Of deaths put on by cunning and forced cause,
> And, in the upshot, purposes mistook
> Fall'n on the'inventors' heads.

And *all this,* he reiterated with sober confidence, could he *truly deliver.* The more we study this speech, the more must we be struck by its specific, detailed and analytical cast. Horatio was not proposing to speak vaguely of horrors, mysteries, wonders all ill-understood; he clearly believed that he had it in his power to achieve a logical elucidation of the whole complex affair.

And yet there is no record of any further activity on

Horatio's part! This enigma I hope that I shall presently be able to solve. There is, of course, one commonly received explanation. Horatio, it is said, went abruptly cagey at the prompting of literary vanity. *Tell my story*, Hamlet had exhorted him. And the form of words which this injunction accidentally took upon Hamlet's lips had the consequence of suggesting to the bookish student from Wittenberg the idea of literary composition. He therefore saved up the inside information which he undoubtedly possessed and declined any further immediate explanation. This theory is, in a manner, borne out by the facts—or so it would appear. There is Horatio's eventual book to witness to it. Let me turn to that for a moment.

*The Life and Letters of Hamlet the Dane, together with Miscellaneous Recollections and Reflections, in six volumes, by Horatio, Lord Chamberlain to his late Sacred Majesty, King Fortinbras of Denmark,* is universally allowed to be a disappointing book. Indeed, to speak quite frankly, I doubt whether so abysmally dull a treatment of a promising subject was to appear again until Bishop Christopher Wordsworth's biography of his Uncle William was published in 1851. Of new light upon the Elsinore affair there is absolutely none. The narrative is wandering and obscure, the arguments adduced are prolix and often self-contradictory, and Hamlet's story is virtually submerged beneath torrents of that tedious moralising which seems almost to have been an occupational disease among Lords Chamberlain at the Danish court.

These may appear to be harsh words. Yet they do no more than match our irritation in face of this wretched state of affairs. It would seem to be undeniable that literary vanity prompted Horatio to sit tight upon his biography of Hamlet until the mists of senescence had closed over his memories and perceptions with all the fatality of those engulfing vapours which enshroud the singularly comfortless castle of Elsinore in Sir Laurence Olivier's film. Well, there is no help for it, and from this barren aspect of our subject we may now turn away. I must warn you, however, that there is one facet of what we may term the Horatio-fiasco to which I shall come back presently.

### III

I think it is very commonly believed that Hamlet's story, having unfortunately come down to us largely through works of entertainment, lies hopelessly obscured beneath the devices of sensational fiction. And most notable among these is that ghost which is declared to have appeared before the young prince on the battlements, announced itself as his father's spirit, and told the dreadful story of fratricide in an orchard. We, who seek to deal with what Dr. Johnson finely calls *vehement real life*, are disconcerted by this appearance in the records of what the same critic terms phantoms that strut upon a stage. In our haste to rationalise the ghost (as we must, of course, do) we rationalise it wrongly. Or so I hope to prove.

The ghost, it is said, was a mere hallucination of Hamlet's—a projecting into the outer world of some disordered inward vision. If we accept this we may well suppose that Claudius's obscure displeasure at *The Murder of Gonzago*, the play which is said to have been presented before him, had nothing to do with a guilty conscience; and that the whole train of events, whatever it may have been, had its origin not in any crime of Claudius's but in a mental aberration of his nephew Hamlet's. Against this very colourable reading of the matter there seems at first little to oppose except certain fragmentary reports that Claudius was subject to fits of religious depression in which he could be heard to confess to some heinous crime. And when we ask why Hamlet should imagine the ghost and its story we are at once assisted by the findings of modern psychology. Hamlet was in the grip of the Œdipus complex, and the ghost and its story were a sort of dream or phantasy, giving body to certain of his own infantile and unconscious desires. The ghost, we may say, was an archetypal father-figure, of a sort generated when the human family was a blood-soaked affair: one of such phantoms as are perpetually rising to haunt us from hiding-places thousands of generations deep.

I will at once admit that this interpretation appears attractive; for if it does not absolutely avoid superstition it at least avoids any superstition that has been current for very long. And yet it appears to me hazardous lightly to swop for this modish phylogenetic phantom the commonplace old ghost of Hamlet's father which the documents in the case so inescapably confront us with. The ghost is eminently a *questionable shape*; if we decline speaking terms with it we cannot claim to be confronting the evidence fairly. For there is much testimony that in the early stages of the affair not only Hamlet himself (whom I have indeed admitted to be of a somewhat unstable nervous constitution) but also a number of substantially disinterested persons—persons, so far as can be ascertained, without previous interest in spiritualism, psychical research, or anything of the sort—were firmly convinced of the nocturnal appearance at Elsinore of a veridical phantasm of the dead. Moreover the phantasm was *heard* by these people; nothing is stronger in the testimony than that they several times heard it utter the word *Swear*—while one account even avers that it was heard not merely to repeat this single

83

word but to deliver a whole sentence: *Swear by his sword*
—a circumstance even more difficult to reconcile with
any theory of simple auditory hallucination.

I cannot, then, accept the theory that there was no
ghost. At the same time I am obliged to believe tha
there was, up to this point, no *crime*. And my grounds for
this are as follows. Everybody who was present at the
playing of *The Murder of Gonzago* concurs in declaring
that Claudius sat quite unmoved through a precise
rehearsal, in the form of a dumb-show, of the play that
was to come. Now, how could he have done this had the
representation been, all unexpectedly, the very picture
of a ghastly fratricidal deed of his own? Moreover, when
he did break up the play he had ample occasion for
doing so in the offensive behaviour of his nephew
Hamlet not only to himself but to a young lady of the
court, Polonius's daughter Ophelia. Thus Hamlet's
"mouse-trap" cannot be held to have caught anything,
and the whole case against Claudius as a criminal
breaks down.

And yet a number of persons claimed to have seen
and heard old King Hamlet's ghost; and from this
apparition Hamlet himself had a substantial account of
his uncle's guilt, coupled with demands for vengeance.
How is this to be explained? If we are to arrive at the
truth we must closely examine the train of events which
this apparently supernatural revelation set in motion.
And particularly we must ask ourselves this question:
whom did this train of events ultimately benefit? It is
perhaps not too much to say that, as soon as I have
asked you this, the first outlines of the truth—the horrible
and surprising truth—begin to form themselves before
you.

Old King Hamlet then was dead, and the succession
to the throne of Denmark had been securely settled. The

monarchy, as you know, was elective in character; and
on this occasion the late king's son, young Hamlet, had
been passed over in favour of an older and altogether
more experienced ruler, the late king's brother, Claudius.
But although young Hamlet may have been in some
discontent about this, there is no reason to suppose that
he was inclined actively to dispute it. For his preoccupa-
tions at this time seem to have been personal in character,
and it was his mother's second marriage (undutiful and
indecently hasty, as he conceived it) that had chief place
in his mind. This no doubt disposed him to think ill of
his Uncle Claudius in general. But state affairs were, as
I say, in a substantially settled condition. It was widely
felt that young Hamlet might yet, in the natural course
of things, succeed to the throne; and Claudius indeed
had in public audience designated him as what we
should call heir presumptive, declaring him to be *most
immediate to his throne . . . his chiefest courtier, cousin, and his
son.*

We must note, however, that Gertrude was by no
means past the child-bearing age, and that if she brought
Claudius a son an alternative strong claim to the succession would thereby be established at once. And who else
might have substantial hopes? Clearly, in an elective
monarchy, the most powerful and politically experienced
of the court nobles—in this case the Lord Chamberlain
Polonius. And, if Polonius, then of course at one farther
remove Polonius's only son, Laertes—whom at one time,
indeed, we know the populace to have shouted for as
king. Was there anyone else? I think it likely that there
was. You will recall that when Polonius's daughter,
Ophelia (having, as it was supposed, committed suicide),
was brought to burial, the priest responsible for the
service plainly regarded the dead girl with extreme
disfavour. Was this solely because suicide was at that

time regarded as mortal sin? I think not. Some other cause must have been operative to make this priest so churlish and venomous. And I suspect, on several grounds, that he had not long before been pressed into service to perform a hasty marriage of a clandestine character. In other words, had Ophelia lived, she might have borne to her secret husband, Prince Hamlet, a child who would also have had a strong claim to the Danish throne. Was there anyone *else* who might have had such a claim? Remember that those were rough old times, and that bastardy was no certain bar to an inheritance or succession. When we admit this, we see at once that Claudius's natural sons, Rosencrantz and Guildenstern, also had their outside chance. They possessed, it must be admitted, all the craft of their father, and do in fact remarkably instance in their characters the power of heredity. I do not think that, at the court of Elsinore, you could have mistaken them for other than what they were.

## IV

And now see what the situation is. All those people, and only those people, die violent and more or less mysterious deaths, who either (1) are on the throne of Denmark (Claudius) or (2) may succeed to it (Hamlet, Polonius, Laertes, Rosencrantz, Guildenstern) or (3) may bear heirs to it (Queen Gertrude, Ophelia). And so we have only to ask ourselves this: who would come to the throne if all these persons were liquidated? The answer is simple: the man who did come to the throne when they were!

I embrace my fortune.
I have some rights of memory in this kingdom,
Which now to claim my vantage doth invite me. . . .

Can we doubt, once we have coolly considered the matter, that Fortinbras of Norway was himself the architect—the diabolically cunning architect—of the *vantage* he so promptly turned up to claim? Just think! No sooner is the way cleared—no sooner are Claudius, Gertrude, Laertes, Hamlet dead or dying, than up pops this fellow who has for months been mysteriously lurking about the environs of Elsinore—up he pops, I say, with an army, and brass band, and a battery of cannon; and he makes a great noise, and a speech announcing that he is the new king; and he has the bodies all carried away in huggermugger, *even while men's minds are wild*, as Horatio innocently puts it. Or is it so innocently, we may ask ourselves? Had Horatio already been squared, and was Fortinbras secure in the knowledge that his future Lord Chamberlain, when it came to the point, would have nothing material to say *to th'yet unknowing world*? Indeed I think I can tell you just when Horatio came into the plot. For when we look back, in the light of all this new knowledge, to the affair of the ghost we see at once that Horatio's whole attitude must be gravely suspect. At the very first recorded appearance of the ghost we catch Horatio prevaricating to the sentinels. And to what end? To no other end than that of persuading them that the supposed ghost is really like the late King Hamlet!

> Such was the very armour he had on,
> When he the ambitious Norway combated,
> So frowned he once, when in an angry parle
> He smote the sledded Polacks on the ice.
> 'Tis strange . . .

Well, it was indeed strange. For we find upon a little calculation that Horatio is here claiming to have been present at an incident which must have taken place when he was in his nursery—young Hamlet having been born, you may remember the reliable testimony of the grave-digger assuring us, on the very day that the ambitious King of Norway was defeated by King Hamlet. And again we know that Horatio only a little later, when endeavouring to persuade Hamlet that the supposed ghost indeed bore a convincing resemblance to the dead king, declared *I knew your father, These hands are not more like*—this only a matter of minutes after admitting that he had seen King Hamlet only once in his life, and that presumably in his own early childhood! I need waste no further words on this. It is painfully evident that when Fortinbras, roughly disguised to represent the ghost of old King Hamlet, took up his perambulations on the battlements of Elsinore, Horatio was already in the plot. No wonder that his book when he finally published it only made obscurity more obscure!

## V

*My hour*—as this false apparition said—*is almost come*, and I need not expatiate on either Fortinbras's motive or opportunity. Remember only that King Hamlet had killed Fortinbras's father and (as the consequence, it was averred, of some obscure wager) possessed himself of a substantial portion of his territories. This was surely ground enough for an implacable resolution to revenge himself upon the Danish royal house. Remember too that young Fortinbras, like young Hamlet, seems to have been cheated of a throne by a usurping uncle, who vexatiously interfered with the young man's military plans. And remember finally that young Fortinbras, by first proposing an expedition against the Danes, and then agreeing to accept safe-conduct from them for the purpose of proceeding against Poland, was able to be right on the spot virtually throughout the whole vexed series of events which we have been elucidating. He was even lurking just round the corner, you will recall, when Hamlet was being shipped off to England; and I do not doubt that his machinations were responsible for both the adventure with the pirates and the surprisingly ruthless course to which Hamlet was prompted by way of liquidating his cousins, Guildenstern and Rosencrantz. For everywhere Fortinbras's intent is plain: it was simply to embroil in mutual suspicion, hatred and strategem all those who stood between him and the throne of Denmark. And so cunningly did he work that (although morally, of course, every fatality in the whole series must be laid wholly to his charge) he was yet himself, in all probability, directly and physically responsible for only one murder: the callous drowning of Ophelia.

And now I fear that I might almost say with Fortinbras:

> The glow-worm shows the matin to be near,
> And 'gins to pale his uneffectual fire.

To trace out this matter further is beyond my present scope, but its outline is tolerably clear. Claudius and Hamlet were alike more sinned against than sinning; and, but for the wiles of a subtle and determined adversary, they would doubtless have come to live together harmoniously enough, once the rather awkward matter of the hasty marriage had had time to settle down. As it was, they were entrapped into killing each other. Further, I will say only this. When I consider the sheer weight of paper and ink rendered obsolete by the simple discovery that I have been privileged to communicate to you to-night I am—let me be not ashamed to confess it—more than a little awed.

# THE FOOL'S SAGA

## *by* RAYNER HEPPENSTALL

First broadcast in two parts on Monday, June 27th, 1949, with the following cast:

| | |
|---|---|
| Hermintrude | JEAN TAYLOR SMITH |
| Godfrey | DUNCAN McINTYRE |
| The Ollave | JOHN LAURIE |
| Feng | MALCOLM HAYES |
| Gertrude | GLADYS YOUNG |
| Hunferth | FREDERICK LLOYD |
| Thora | JOAN HART |
| Tosti | ESME PERCY |
| Hamlet | DAVID KING-WOOD |
| Cimbal | RAF DE LA TORRE |
| Carvel | EDWARD FORSYTH |
| Balant | BRYAN POWLEY |
| Fyris | DIANA MADDOX |
| Minimus | JOHN GLYN-JONES |
| Drafnar | BASIL DIGNAM |
| Hugh | BASIL JONES |
| Wiglek | ALASTAIR DUNCAN |

The music was composed by William Wordsworth and played by the B.B.C. Theatre Orchestra under Walter Goehr, with Jeanne Chevreau (harp) and Martin Boddey (tenor).

# INTRODUCTION

IF YOU READ the prefatory note to almost any edition of *Hamlet*, you will learn that Shakespeare based his tragedy on a lost play by Kyd, that Kyd took the story from a French writer, Belleforest, and that Belleforest merely embroidered the tale as it occurs in the Danish chronicles of Saxo Grammaticus, a priest of the late twelfth century. There is a later Icelandic saga in which everything is fantasticated beyond recognition, and in the literatures and common speech of England, Wales and Ireland there are what appear to be references to the same royal fool, for "Amleth" means "fool." In the West Riding, for instance, there is an expression "to play Hamlet with," which means to cause havoc among, and the word "havoc" in its turn reminds us of another Dane, Havelock, who lived at Grimsby and had much the same kind of degraded childhood. In Latin, "Brutus" means "fool," and Saxo Grammaticus certainly took some elements of his story from the life of the Roman first consul.

Well now, Saxo is not completely unknown. Only a fortnight after I had begun work on this programme, I read in a newspaper that Sir Laurence Olivier had been reading him aloud to members of our own royal family. A wealth of scholarship has grown up about the whole subject, and I must acknowledge a debt to more than one writer on that confused and shadowy age which followed the breakdown of the Roman Empire and which the history books call "the period of migrations," for if we try to get back to the Hamlet behind Saxo Grammaticus, that is where we find ourselves, somewhere late in the fifth or at the beginning of the sixth century. Hamlet must have been roughly contemporary with Beowulf, a little later than St. Patrick. Hengist and Horsa had settled in the Isle of Thanet. The Saxons were creeping up our east coast. The Scots, from Ireland, seem to have occupied the coasts of what is now Scotland and of Wales and then to have been driven out by Cunedda, war-lord of Britain, who was himself forced to evacuate parts of Scotland in about A.D. 410 because the Picts were pushing south. It is here that pure conjecture begins.

A large part of Hamlet's story is connected with two visits he paid to this country, for there was no happy encounter with pirates to restore him to Elsinore within a few days (in any case, it wasn't Elsinore). Because of this, we have to localise and name a king of Britain and his daughter. We have to localise a Scottish queen, who is given the German name "Hermintrude." Suppose that Hamlet's first journey took place in the year 500. Then either this queen was a queen in Ireland, or she was not Scottish but Pictish. It is argued by Kemp Malone that she was in fact neither, that she was a Gaul captured on a Viking raid by quite another hero and that she had nothing to do with Hamlet at all, that indeed there was no Hamlet. The case is rather a good one, but I prefer to send Kemp Malone packing as a spoil-sport. Now, Britain did not stop short at the south wall. The Picts came a long way south at the beginning of the fifth century, but they seem not to have stayed. There were Britons in Strathclyde fifty years later, and it is not at all unlikely that the last but one of the twelve victorious battles of King Arthur restored the Cymry to Edinburgh and the Lothians, the one territory properly settled by Picts this side of the north wall, in or about the year 516. So, both Hamlet's Britain and Hamlet's Pictland must have lain within the confines of the kingdom formed long afterwards by the union of four peoples under that Duncan who was slain in battle by his general, Macbeth. For no particularly good reason except that it makes her seem less far away, let Hermintrude reign in Edinburgh

94

itself over the Black Brithwyr of the Lothians. And let the British king hold the small and vulnerable territory of Catraeth (here I follow Skene) between Manau Gododin and Pictland proper, lying along the north wall and the south bank of the Forth from Queensferry upstream to Stirling, with advanced fortifications at Caer Eiddyn (Caredin, the eastern extremity of the north wall), his capital Aeron at the mouth of the Avon and a good harbour at Grangemouth for ships from Jutland sailing up the firth. The two days' battle may then be imagined to take place where the last of King Arthur's twelve victorious battles took place twenty years later, at the foot of the Mons Badonis, not Bath but Bathgate, not Badon but Bouden Hill. Was Arthur related to Saxo Grammaticus's British king? Did he fight over this territory to avenge him? And was Modred, son of Lug, allied not perhaps with Saxons, but with Danes, who must have seemed much the same kind of people to the Cymry and who indeed *were* much the same kind of people—was he carrying on this feud when, in A.D. 537, he slew Britain's greatest legendary hero at Arthur's O'on or Camelon? Perhaps this is carrying the love of heresy for its own sake too far. And no conjecture yields us the *name* of Saxo's British king. One would like it to be "Cymbeline." There were three Cymbelines in this part of the world, one in the family tree of Dyfnwal Hen, two in that of Coel, the elder of these perhaps Shakespeare's sweet sovereign, the younger a son of Cynwyd Cynwydion and brother to the only prince associated by his name with precisely that tongue of land we have chosen to thrust into the cheek of Manau Gododin. But, since other evidence shows Clyddno Eiddyn to have been contemporary with the four kings who fought against the sons of Ida, young Cymbeline must have come too late to be acquainted with Hamlet.

95

And so I have done what Shakespeare himself always did; taken names from quite different characters in other books I happened to be reading at the time. If they turned out not to be Cymric, that wouldn't have troubled the master of us all. Consider the names in Shakespeare's *Hamlet*—"Claudius" and "Polonius," "Laertes," "Bernardo," "Rosenkrantz" and "Guildenstern," "Osric," "Fortinbras"—Latin, Greek, Italian, bastard German, English and pseudo-French. At least "Balant" sounds vaguely Celtic, and "Fyris" is pretty. Both these names come from the Icelandic *Ambales Saga*. So do "Godfrey," "Tosti," "Cimbal" and "Carvel," all but "Godfrey" with some appropriateness. "Thora" comes from an earlier book of Saxo's Danish chronicles. Students of Old English will not need to inquire why I have fetched the wretched, rash, intruding fool from another court and called him "Hunferth."

But it is in the writing of dialogue that scholarship gives one least help. We know exactly five words of Pictish plus some proper names of kings. Five words are enough to keep a scholar happy, but I had to write twenty thousand words of dialogue for actors to speak. The language of the Picts may or may not have been intermediate between Gaelic and Brythonic. Whatever else it may have resembled, it cannot have been the Anglian dialect of Robert Burns. With the Britons, already Christianised, there is not much difficulty. All one needs is restraint. Since my own county is as Danish as any part of the kingdom, my plebeian Danes speak broad Yorkshire. Some of my fellow countrymen will accuse me of a lack of piety in not accepting the equation of Catraeth with Catterick. But in other respects, too, it is the Picts of whom we know least. They have been thought to come from Scythia or Greece. They have been identified with the Irish fairy-race of Sidhe and

96

with the Fenians. Except that poety was more highly esteemed than it is to-day, the manners and customs of the age of migrations were unedifying. Among great families, polygamy seems to have been general. The Picts are even accused of cannibalism, though a more heinous crime, in the eyes of the Christian Britons, appears to have been that they were not content with honest mead or ale. In tones of trembling indignation, they are called "distillers." Perhaps that explains the purpose of those mysterious structures known as vitrified forts.

But the great underlying struggle of the age was the same as that which, if we are to believe Mr. James Thurber, divides America to-day. Perhaps it was that, with so much indiscriminate slaughter on every hand, men had begun to acquire a scarcity value. At any rate, a patriarchal form of society had not completely ousted matrilineal succession and worship of the female principle, but gods were everywhere driving out goddesses, and the new gospel completed this process. My Pictish Queen, in many ways all too human, is also a goddess. I have not remained uninfluenced by some recent speculations of a living poet (Mr. Graves), but I would also point out that Goethe once thought of writing a play on the saga Hamlet, and Goethe had his own cult of the eternal feminine, "*das ewig Weibliche*." If it is complained that I have been unnecessarily crude in matters connected with either love or battle, I shall appeal to my sources, and I shall say too, unfair as it may seem after I have dismissed him, that, according to Kemp Malone, the original legend contained elements far more horrible than those I have retained—for instance, a mangled body purporting to be Hamlet's and the rape of a true sister not in feigned but in authentic bestiality. *Ambales Saga* contains hints for the notion that Hamlet belonged to a glandular type which may seem imbecile in youth.

# THE FOOL'S SAGA

[*Edinburgh.* A.D. *490. Late spring. The Pictish queen receives in audience a spy and ten soldiers, who have brought to her a shield in painted wood and a wooden tablet which is in fact a letter. Beside her, in this barbarically ornate throne-room, stands her* OLLAVE, *or master-poet.*

HERMINTRUDE: Frae whom?

GODFREY: Frae Balant.

HERMINTRUDE: And what says he?

GODFREY: I canna read, my lady. The news is that Balant seeks to unite the twa kingdoms by a marriage.

HERMINTRUDE: Here . . .

OLLAVE: It is set out in a vile mingling of Latin characters and ogham, my lady, but doubtless I could——

HERMINTRUDE: And the shield?

OLLAVE: The runes are Danish, from Jutland. The drawings—ay, very delicate, very——

HERMINTRUDE: Them I can see. What does the British king write?

OLLAVE: His ollave, or rather his bard or *pencerdd*, or perhaps a monk from Gaul, writes, in accord with the news of this worthy blinker, that his master, King Balant, begs in wedlock the white hand of the Pictish queen Hermintrude and that these Danes are his ambassadors. The young king, their leader, is his son-in-law——

HERMINTRUDE: Mm?

OLLAVE: —wedded to—

HERMINTRUDE: His name?

OLLAVE: God, man, water, fir-tree, giant. His name is Hamlet.

HERMINTRUDE: And here on the shield——?

OLLAVE: In these wee figures, his life is porturate, beginning with the death of the man's father.

HERMINTRUDE: Set the shield down, here.

GODFREY: Again this——?

OLLAVE: Gar twa o thae breith kemps hold it, my lady.

HERMINTRUDE: Do as I say.

[*They set down the shield.*

HERMINTRUDE: Now. . . .

GODFREY: You, and you.

GUARDS: My lady.

[*They step forward.*

99

OLLAVE: There. No, up a little and to the left.

HERMINTRUDE: Straighten your arm.

GUARDS: My lady.

OLLAVE: There. So the rayons o the setting sun fall upon it, and till evening we may scan the shield at leisure, while——

HERMINTRUDE: As to King Balant and his suit of marriage——

OLLAVE: \
GODFREY: / My lady?

HERMINTRUDE: How many *young* men have contented me?

OLLAVE (*hushed*): None.

HERMINTRUDE: Good poets are rare. I let you live.

OLLAVE (*reverential*): Celest, preluciand. . . .

HERMINTRUDE: Two visiting princes have gone away safe. The lave, like the queen bee, the female spider and the praying mantis, I spat forth dead at my chamber door in the morning. Is Balant tired of this world? But I desire not the embraces of old men, their blood half-congealed, their lives flickering in the socket, Kings of Britain, High Kings of Ireland, Anglian pirates or Phœnician merchants, although . . .

OLLAVE: This King of Jutland is young.

HERMINTRUDE: And fair?

GODFREY: No, black or rather——

HERMINTRUDE: A black Dane?

GODFREY: He is dark as a Greek.

HERMINTRUDE: His story, then. Keep the shield still.

GUARDS: My lady.

OLLAVE: Here, at the top——

HERMINTRUDE: Two bearded men with swords uplifted. A third falls. So?

OLLAVE: Gin the Danes fight in single combat or *holmgang*, they row out to an island in the river mouth and there——

HERMINTRUDE: This is ambush, not single combat. The two waited under the porch on either side the folding doors.

OLLAVE: That is true, yes. One is the brother of this murdered man. His name . . . Gold, sapling-fir . . .

HERMINTRUDE: Well?

OLLAVE: I trace the runes. Money, fir-tree, hero. His name is Feng. He who falls is Orwendill, the father of Hamlet. He slew the frost-king. Orwendill is a god of the returning sun, a spring-god, Lug——

HERMINTRUDE: Then Hamlet is divine.

OLLAVE: As the Danes reckon divinity. Orwendill falls in a winter wood. Hamlet must slay his uncle, Feng. But Hamlet is black-avised and puts on madness. The people doubt him. Feng allows him to live.

HERMINTRUDE: Here, in bed——?

OLLAVE: Gertrude or Geruth, mother of Hamlet——

HERMINTRUDE: And Feng. Gertrude——?

OLLAVE: Her father is the High King of Denmark, Roderick Ringslinger.

HERMINTRUDE: So the crown is in any case not Hamlet's——

OLLAVE: I——

HERMINTRUDE: —unless——

OLLAVE: The Danes have strange views on succession, great queen. There, it is the son who succeeds his father.

HERMINTRUDE: You dare, fellow, to——?

OLLAVE: I mock you not, goddess of the moon and the underworld. These fair-haired, garter-breeked Teutons, with their battle-axes, their long keels, living in great barns, sleeping on benches in the mead-hall, they entertain, believe me, lady the wildest, the most outrageous beliefs. Their ollaves or scalds are the finest in the world for war-poetry and the sea (I wish I could say as much for their jewellers who seem unable to think of anything to do with gold but twist it) but they do not well ken that authority is uterine. Indeed, it is not wholly phallic either with them, for if the succession fall into dispute the men assemble together in a field and settle the matter with their lungs.

HERMINTRUDE: Yet some among them need to feign madness?

OLLAVE: The principle seems to work in some mysterious way. Their women are not slaves, either. It is true, these tribes are always at war.

HERMINTRUDE: And so those two in bed, Gertrude and Feng, hope to beget a son.

OLLAVE: That may be surmised. I ought perhaps to add that marriage with a husband's brother is regarded by the Danes as incest. The matter of succession apart, Hamlet would therefore feel some justifiable resentment. Indeed, it may have turned his mind a little, though what follows——

HERMINTRUDE: I hae seen just such young men at court. Creish and silent in childhood, horribly moved in adolescence, at the age of a man they grew lean and of steady temper. Men like these—but do forth.

OLLAVE: Here, Feng is troubled. He seeks proof.

HERMINTRUDE: Of what?

OLLAVE: This is the queen's bride-bower. The bower-maidens——

HERMINTRUDE: This third figure——?

OLLAVE: One of Feng's older thanes, his counsellor, or——

GODFREY: My lady——

HERMINTRUDE: Well?

GODFREY: I think his name was Hunferth.

OLLAVE: Again this is the news?

GODFREY: It is bruited. He was sent from Zealand, Roderick's spokesman, the Ringslinger.

HERMINTRUDE: I hear the laughter of the bower-maidens. The spinning wheel clatters, the shuttle is passed frae hand to hand across the loom. The folding doors are thrown open.

[*These sounds have gradually become audible. We are now in* QUEEN GERTRUDE's *bride-bower in Jutland, and it is the spring of* A.D. 489.

FENG (*he is a rather stupid man and at the moment very much on edge*): Silence!

HUNFERTH: Silence! Silence!

GERTRUDE (*more intelligent, less rattled, but nervously uncertain of where her loyalty lies*): Silence!

[*She claps her hands. The chattering stops.*

GERTRUDE: The king——

HUNFERTH: The under-king. . . . I beg your pardon, my lady.

104

GERTRUDE: The king wishes to speak to you. Speak to them, Feng.

FENG: Which of you was fostered with Hamlet?

1ST BOWER-MAIDEN: Go on. You were.

2ND BOWER-MAIDEN: Yes, go on. Speak up, Thora.

FENG: Well?

THORA: I was.

[*Renewed whispering.*

GERTRUDE: Yes, yes, her mother. I remember now.

HUNFERTH: A comely child. At the court of the high king——

GERTRUDE: Well?

FENG: This girl should serve the turn, Gertrude.

GERTRUDE: She is both fair and froward.

THORA: My lady!

FENG: What is your name, child?

THORA: Thora.

[*The whispering becomes noisier. There are giggles.*

HUNFERTH: Silence! Silence!

FENG: Silence!

[*It stops.*

105

FENG: You have seen how the Lord Hamlet sits all day in the kitchen-stead, raking the cinders with his hands, feeding on swill, his face and body filthy, his mind listless.

BOWER-MAIDENS: Yes, we have seen him. It is true.

FENG: This is great shame in a prince. This black hulk, this block, this slobbering glutton, with his virgin's voice——

GERTRUDE: Hamlet is my son, Feng, and a great lord.

HUNFERTH: My lord, my lord, the high king Roderick's grandson, kin of the Ringslinger. . . .

FENG: You speak, Gertrude.

GERTRUDE: The king and I are much tried by Hamlet's listlessness. The hands of a king's son should be busied with the bow, the sword and the spear, with horses and keels——

FENG: Instead of sharpening wood spits and hardening them in the fire, nobody knows what for.

HUNFERTH: My lord, this is not for the ears of these bower-maidens.

GERTRUDE: It may be that some love of women could mend him.

HUNFERTH: Ay. In the time of the old King Hrothgar, I call to mind——

GERTRUDE: Or it may be——

FENG: Men have put on madness out of guile.

GERTRUDE: Be careful what you say, Feng.

FENG: Has any of you—this is what I want to know . . .

[*Whispering stops. He suddenly blusters.*

FENG: Has any of you ever lain with the Lord Hamlet?

[*Silence.*

FENG (*angrily*): Well?

BOWER-MAIDENS: No, my lord, never. No, none of us.

GERTRUDE: Feng!

1ST BOWER-MAIDEN: He would spurn us, my lord.

2ND BOWER-MAIDEN: The Prince flouts all young women,
Feng.

THE OTHERS: No, he's not fond of girls. Hamlet's not
one for kissing, my lord.

HUNFERTH: The under-king would say, has the Lord
Hamlet never yet stretched out a hand to your skirts
or——

FENG: In that hovel of his which he keeps blocked up
with a stone——

GERTRUDE: It's no use asking them.

FENG: No. You, girl. . . .

HUNFERTH: You, his foster-sister, Thora. . . .

THORA: Yes, Feng?

FENG: Go to the great hall. No. No, perhaps I'd best——

GERTRUDE: Feng, it is my son she is to trap, not my husband.

FENG: The great hall, girl.

THORA: Yes, Feng.

HUNFERTH: Go, then, Thora. At the court of the high king, they would——

GERTRUDE: You others, if my son speaks to you, do what you can to bring him out of this mood. And if you witness anything untoward, anything which worries you, tell it to me.

HUNFERTH: Or if the queen is not to be found, I will hear it. You may——

BOWER-MAIDENS: Yes, my lady. We shall.

FENG: Hamlet has a great wound across his back.

GERTRUDE: Feng——

FENG: How did he get it? Where does he fare at night with the outlaw Drafnar and the vile dwarf, Tosti?

HUNFERTH: My lord, these are not bride-bower matters.

FENG (*woodenly*): No.

HUNFERTH: Come, girl.

GERTRUDE: The rest of you busy yourselves with hangings for the great hall.

BOWER-MAIDENS: Yes, my lady. We have our patterns.

GERTRUDE: Come, then.

FENG: Ay, we'll see to the bottom of this madness.

HUNFERTH: I recall, in the time of the high King Hrothgar, when that ambitious young man from the tip of Sweden, Beowulf—he'll rule here in Denmark yet, mark my words—was brought in to deal with the giant Grendel and his mother. . . .

[*Their voices recede, and we are again in the Pictish throne-room, where the first sounds we hear are the shield clattering to the floor and the slap of* HERMINTRUDE'S *hand across a guard's face.*

OLLAVE: Tentless!

GODFREY: Steady man!

1ST GUARD (*almost in tears*): My fingers were crampit, lady. My arm——

109

HERMINTRUDE: We'll chop them off. How old are you?

1ST GUARD: Seventeen, my lady.

OLLAVE: And ye canna hold a shield ten minutes together? Nay, man——

GODFREY: He's a good swordsman, my lady.

HERMINTRUDE: I bade neither of you speak. Tak up the shield.

GUARDS: Ay, my lady.

HERMINTRUDE: Give it to the ollave.

OLLAVE: Great queen, I——

HERMINTRUDE: Now, man, you——

GODFREY: Great queen.

HERMINTRUDE: Dismiss these ten. The shanks o the others will need stretching too. They look underfed. Let them watch, as the shadows lengthen. Let them bring here a who stray alone frae this embassy.

GODFREY: My lady. Day guard, to the left, turn. Right, man, spear on your shoulder. Quick march.

HERMINTRUDE: Set it down, there. There, against the pillar. Now spell on. How is the girl put to work? I see the next scene is a hunt. And there is Hamlet sitting back to front on his horse.

OLLAVE: More feigned madness. This gaping wolf——

HERMINTRUDE: What is that sticking out of the sand?

OLLAVE: That is the rudder of a wrecked ship. The young thanes, Hamlet's companions, are mocking him. They say that it is a knife. And he, that it is the right thing to carve that huge ham, the sea.

HERMINTRUDE: I have seen just such a rudder stranded, here in the firth. It was very like a great whittle. What else does he say?

OLLAVE: That the wolf is a young colt and that in his uncle's stud there are too few of that kind fighting.

HERMINTRUDE: A riddling madness.

OLLAVE: They say to him that the sand is meal. And he, that the ocean ground it small. But indeed, my lady, this is now part of the poets' world, like your own pre-celling, blench majesty and the alphabet of trees. For the Danish god of the sea is Ægir, whom we call by his Greek name Okeanos, or Leir, and his nine daughters grind at the mill which Hamlet called the skerry-quern, because of all the rocky islets in the western sea.

HERMINTRUDE: The world's a mill.

OLLAVE: My lady?

HERMINTRUDE: The eyes are hollowed by the attrition of tears. The heart contracts. The sword sings, and the heads fall. The grass withers, and the dykes are blown wide.

OLLAVE (*hushed*): Venust, preclair. . . . It is so indeed. And thus Hamlet speaks upon the sea-coast of Jutland.

HERMINTRUDE: And the girl, his foster-sister, this Thora?

OLLAVE: She walks by herself at the sea's edge, toward the dunes. The bower-maidens are gathering dulse and lava-weed. They stand in the sea, their skirts picked up above their knees. She goes apart and walks barefooted beyond the headland. Hamlet's companions guide him toward where they know she is and leave him, but, creeping behind the dunes and parting the dry grasses, watch. Here I cannot tell what is being done. I read "gadfly," "warning," "a distant fen," "and there he lay with her." That night, in the great hall of Feng, at the ale-bench in Jutland, under cover of the harping and the saga-telling, a new saga begins.

[*We hear the stir of a banquet, with noisy conversation and laughter. In the background,* TOSTI *declaims to the harp throughout.*

TOSTI: Helgi slew Hodbrodd,     whose son Hother
grew up in grace,     Gewar's fosterling,
still a stripling,     outstood in strength
to stride or strike     or play upon strings.
To Hother's harping     Nanna hearkened,
a girl-child of Gewar,     in love's gladness,
eyed his archery.     Ah, but another
beheld her bathing,     Odin's son Baldur,
fain of her fair body,     his blood on fire,
would hack down Hother     and have for his own
this girl, a demi-god.     He told Gewar
how it stood with him.     Hother out hunting
strayed in a mist,     on a house struck

where in whispers      he was taught by wood-maidens
Baldur's longing for     the boy's foster-sister,
in a fog-building     by framers of battle.
It melted away.     Only Miming, . . .

YOUNG THANES: Ssh! Ssh! Here she is.

1ST YOUNG THANE: Where's Hamlet?

2ND YOUNG THANE: Did he lie with her?

CIMBAL: He told us he did. Now we've lost him again.

CARVEL: He's up on the fell with trolls, dwarfs and outlaws.

3RD YOUNG THANE: Have you spoken to Thora?

1ST YOUNG THANE: Did she weep?

2ND YOUNG THANE: Did she say he'd robbed her boot-lessly, for no blood-fee would make good what she had lost?

CIMBAL: She denies all.

3RD YOUNG THANE: Did he——?

CARVEL: We asked him where he lay with her. He said upon the hoof of a beast of burden——

1ST YOUNG THANE: What?

CARVEL: Upon a cockscomb——

113

YOUNG THANES: A cockscomb!

CIMBAL: And upon rafters.

[*They shout with laughter.*

CARVEL: There's Feng now. He'll want to know.

CIMBAL: Ay.

1ST YOUNG THANE: Come, we'll talk to Thora.

YOUNG THANES: Ay, come along.

TOSTI: . . . for no steel might slay     the Wanderer's son,
had blade and bracelet     to harm Baldur,
a witch of the woods.     This dread warlock
over the ice     to a cave in the hillside,
with his tent and tackle     and a reindeer team,
Hother hunted     through the hard weather.
Fell a shadow.     Miming, shackled,
Gave up his gear.     Then did Gelder
sail from Saxony,     told and seeking
what Hother 'd hid.     The youthful hero
subdued the Saxon,     sailed in service
with tongue-tied Helgi     of Halogaland,
Fought with the Finns.     While he thus fared
Odin's son armed himself,     entered on Gewar
to sue for Nanna,     who sent him answer
a god with a girl     could not together. . . .

1ST BOWER-MAIDEN: Why didn't you tell him to pray to
Frigga for guidance?

2ND BOWER-MAIDEN: I'd sooner a man in his right mind.

1ST YOUNG THANE: Here's one!

1ST BOWER-MAIDEN: Let go. Gertrude's watching you.

3RD YOUNG THANE: They'll have it out of you by trial.

BOWER-MAIDENS: No, no!

1ST YOUNG THANE: They'll have their old men's thumbs about your dugs.

BOWER-MAIDENS: Oh, don't listen to them, Thora! No, no, no!

THORA: I tell you, he didn't touch me. He did nothing.

3RD YOUNG THANE: *We* believe you, but——

2ND YOUNG THANE: What are Feng and the Ringslinger's counsellor talking about?

TOSTI: . . . join or enjoy.    Hother engendered
Roderick whose rings    rolled in the sea,
fell short of his champion.    Four times in a fray
Hother encountered    the son of Odin,
on the fourth felled him.    With Boe he failed.
These are the deeds    of Hodbrodd's son
and Baldur's bane.    He broke Thor's hammer,
hewing it off at the haft.    The gods he hurled down,
he set the Saxon    on a pyre of ships.
Hother hastened to    Nanna's embraces,
avenged her father.    A snake-venom,
halting with his harp,    he had from the wood-maidens,
Bread of Baldur.    In a royal barrow
slept Odin's son. . . .

FENG: His mother?

HUNFERTH: I'll hide myself and listen.

FENG: I can't hear. This dreary tale of Baldur and Hother. Tell him to stop.

HUNFERTH: Peace, good dwarf. Peace, I say.

TOSTI: Eh? Nay, the King told me——

FENG: Quiet, you twisted fool, or I'll have them pelt you with beef-bones.

HUNFERTH: Feng, it is unwise to gain a bad name from poets.

FENG: Mm. Stay. Here's a bracelet.

[*A bracelet rings on the floor.*]

TOSTI: I thank you, great King.

FENG: We'll hear another tale later. Now what did you say?

HUNFERTH: I'll hide myself and give ear.

FENG: Is it safe? For Gertrude, I mean?

HUNFERTH: He'll trust one who bore him.

FENG: As soon as the ladies leave us, then. We'll say that I am called to Elsinore this very night. Now find Hamlet. The girl too. Face to face. I'll find out which of them is telling the truth.

HUNFERTH: Feng, if you take my counsel——

FENG: Go, I tell you! Go!

———————

GERTRUDE: Hamlet, put off this lumpish mood. The time to mourn is over.

HAMLET: Cock-a-doodle-doo.

GERTRUDE: Hamlet, I rejoice to hear that you went out hunting this afternoon. You should go out more. It is spring. The beech-trees are budded. The new-pitched keels tug at their moorings. You need——

HAMLET: Cock-a-doodle-doo.

GERTRUDE: What do you say, Hamlet?

HAMLET: The bride-bower is full of clean rushes, mother. They are ill-strewn, there are too many in the far corner. What are you hoping to hide? My father's blood——?

GERTRUDE: Hamlet——

HAMLET: Or your own whoredom? Cock-a-doodle-doo.

GERTRUDE: Hamlet——

HAMLET: I say, Cock-a-doodle-doo! The old cock is off to Zealand, so I'll crow. Look, I beat my wings, mother.

GERTRUDE: Hamlet——

HAMLET: I'll go pick over this clean straw to see if I can find my father. Cock-a-doodle-doo! Cock-a-doodle-doo! . . .

117

GERTRUDE: Hamlet! Hamlet! Come here, I beg of you. There is nothing there. Hamlet, I swear to you! Hamlet, your mother!

HAMLET: Cock-a-doodle-doo! Cock-a-doodle-doo! Cock-a-doodle——

HUNFERTH: Ha!

HAMLET: Come out!

HUNFERTH: My lord, my lord!

GERTRUDE: Hamlet! Hamlet!

HAMLET: And out, sword! There . . . and there . . . and there . . . and there!

HUNFERTH: Ah! . . . My Lord, my lord! . . . Ha! . . . Ha! . . .

[*He dies.*

GERTRUDE: Hamlet! . . . Hamlet! . . . Oh, Hamlet! . . . Oh. . . .

[*She breaks down and sobs.*

HAMLET: So, mother, you are Feng's whore and his spy too.

GERTRUDE: Oh, Hamlet, this is madness indeed.

HAMLET: Vilest of women! Do you think, then, to hide so heavy a guilt under a straw grief? Oh, unclean!

118

GERTRUDE: Hamlet, your father——

HAMLET: Feng killed your husband—he and another lay in wait for him in the shadow of his own lintel, on either side his threshold—and you wanton with him. He spilled my father's blood, and you woo him with little cries to these sheets, to nuzzle in these breasts that fed me.

GERTRUDE: Hamlet!

HAMLET: Thus——

GERTRUDE: Hamlet!

HAMLET: Nay, listen, mother. Thus do mares couple with the stallion that trampled their master.

GERTRUDE: Ah!

HAMLET: They are brute beasts, they know no better. But you, a queen of men! I have put on madness. Feng cut down his brother. A bootless crime: there is no blood-fee for a brother. Feng should have hung side by side with a live wolf, if there had been a law in Jutland. He will cut me down when he fears me enough, if I am not too spry for him, mother. And that I will be. I will avenge my father.

GERTRUDE: Ah, no!

HAMLET: There is a time to seem dull and a time for the sword to leap into brightness. Mother, mother, weep not for my witlessness, weep for the darkness in your own mind. Think of that which is done and that which is still to do. And say nothing, nothing. Do you hear, mother?

GERTRUDE: I hear you, Hamlet.

HAMLET: Keep all this hidden.

GERTRUDE: I will, I will.

HAMLET: I fear not the fang of Feng! Now I'll get rid of my ill-pitching grandfather's too-willing counsellor. How pale he is, how still. I'll to the jakes with him, hew him up small and simmer him, swill him out to the pigs. Time has not moved since he was a man, and now he's none. I fear you'll need more clean rushes, mother. His blood still runs, and yet there are no thoughts stirring in his mind. His heart trots after no master now.

---

DRAFNAR: By Odin, I'll dig the tattoo marks out of your dirty Pictish foreheads.

HUGH: By Llyr, this is no way to treat ambassadors. . . .

GODFREY: Hold the big fellow. Two of you will do for the Briton. Hold him, hold him.

1ST GUARD: Twist that left arm behind his back.

2ND GUARD: I canna get my hands round his great wrist.

1ST GUARD: If a Danes are like this, 'twill tak the queen's whole army tae subdue their embassy.

2ND GUARD: Watch out. He's got the ither han free.

HERMINTRUDE: So, we have a prisoner.

OLLAVE: We have indeed, my lady.

HERMINTRUDE: Who is this?

GODFREY: This is one of the Danes, great queen. The other is one of King Balant's men. The Dane——

HERMINTRUDE: Bring him before us. Quiet, man. I am the queen.

[DRAFNAR *utters a contemptuous* "Ha!"—*then, as he looks at her, a long-drawn* "Oh!" *of appreciation.*

HERMINTRUDE: It seems, young man, that you will dig the tattoo marks out of our——?

OLLAVE: Our dirty Pictish foreheads, my lady.

HERMINTRUDE: Ay. Our forehead, fellow, is not tattooed. (*Voluptuously, as she draws back her sleeve*) Our arm, you see, is.

DRAFNAR: Ay, lady. Ay.

HERMINTRUDE (*briskly*): And there is more. Your name?

DRAFNAR: Drafnar.

OLLAVE: And quality?

DRAFNAR: I am blood-brother to the King of Jutland.

HERMINTRUDE: Let me see, you sprinkle your footprints, do you not, with each other's blood and then stand hand in hand beneath a turf arch? Does this require any special gift or advantage of birth?

DRAFNAR: I helped Hamlet to his revenge. I was an outlaw in the time of his——

HERMINTRUDE: We are not surprised. But go on.

DRAFNAR: The jet-faxed, pallid queen has a bitter, red tongue.

HERMINTRUDE: I do not mock young men of a strength like yours. Not at the first.

OLLAVE (*whispering*): It may be that this Drafnar——

HERMINTRUDE: Bring the Dane a chair.

GODFREY: My lady.

HERMINTRUDE: And bid the other prisoner approach. One of King Balant's men.

HUGH: Indeed, your majesty, I——

HERMINTRUDE: Stand here, by the ollave. Now, Drafnar, sit here and gaze with us at this——

DRAFNAR: King Hamlet's shield!

HERMINTRUDE: My spy took it from beneath his sleeping head. My ollave and I were scanning its pictures and its —what do you call these characters?

OLLAVE: Its runes.

HERMINTRUDE: But sit down. We had come to the dispatch of—his name was——?

122

OLLAVE: According to this fellow, Hunferth.

DRAFNAR: Ay, the long-nosed old busybody. Hamlet——

[*He cannot go on. He shouts with laughter at the recollection.*

HERMINTRUDE: Well?

OLLAVE: Come, man.

DRAFNAR: ——dragged him to the kitchen-stead, minced him up small on a butcher's bench and stewed him in a cauldron. Then he——

[*But he is again helpless.*

OLLAVE: We know this, man.

DRAFNAR: Hamlet used to sit all day among the carlines of the kitchen-stead, spoiling the food and sharpening the little crooks he——

OLLAVE: Ah!

DRAFNAR: ——used for his revenge, on Feng's friends. He swilled the aged Hunferth out with the garbage.

OLLAVE: And the swine ate him. That we know.

HERMINTRUDE (*gently*): Drafnar. . . .

DRAFNAR (*apologetic*): My tongue felt the spur, lady. You——?

HERMINTRUDE: What is being done here?

123

DRAFNAR: What, when Thora was set to waylay Hamlet on the dunes?

HERMINTRUDE: Gif her name be Thora.

DRAFNAR: Why, that was a device of Tosti's, to warn him that——

HERMINTRUDE: Tosti?

DRAFNAR: The dwarf. Hamlet rescued his daughter from a troll-woman. That was before he got this great wound on his back from the cave-dweller, Actamund. Ay, Hamlet learned swordsmanship in a rough school, out on the fells at night.

HERMINTRUDE: This Tosti?

DRAFNAR: He knew that Cimbal and Carvel were following Hamlet among the dunes. He fitted a chip of straw to the hinder-parts of a gad-fly, chased it——

OLLAVE: So Tosti was a poet too?

DRAFNAR: Ay, belike. They used him to tell tales in the mead-hall. Well, this gad-fly buzzed around Hamlet and the girl, and Hamlet took it for a warning and carried her down a creek among the salt flats and there he——

HERMINTRUDE: And then, after the murder of Hunferth?

DRAFNAR: Eh? Oh, Hamlet sailed for Britain. That was his first roving. Feng sent Cimbal and Carvel, cringing rogues both of them, to——

OLLAVE: These are Cimbal and Carvel?

DRAFNAR: Like enough. They bore a tablet to this British King, Balant. Hamlet bade me look after his pointed spits. I stored them in his hovel, rolled a great stone to the door. He'd said they were javelins to avenge his father, but the young thanes laughed. His mother he bade weave hangings for the great hall. A year after his going, she was to proclaim his death, and then she was to see what would happen. So they sailed. They came to Britain. I stayed in the hollows and on the fells. Feng would have had me killed. Hamlet's foster-sister fled with me, Thora. The King Balant. . . . But here, this fellow can tell you better than I.

OLLAVE: The shield tells much, my lady.

HERMINTRUDE: Nay, let the Briton speak.

HUGH : 'Twas so, then, great queen. The lords Cimbal and Carvel bore a letter on wood to my master, King Balant. The lord Carvel had visited Britain before.

DRAFNAR: Carvel joined Feng in the murder of his brother, Hamlet's father. Together they lay in wait for Orwendill, with sword arm bent.

HUGH: King Feng had come roving to this land while his brother reigned. He and King Balant, blood-brothers they were.

HERMINTRUDE: Ha?

DRAFNAR: Balant had sprinkled his prints with Feng? Then——?

OLLAVE: This makes all plain.

HERMINTRUDE: Go on, Briton.

HUGH: In this letter, Feng commended to Balant——

DRAFNAR: Com-——?

HUGH: ——commended to him the youth of great judgment who came with the lords Cimbal and Carvel and begged him to give this youth in marriage the hand of his daughter Fyris.

HERMINTRUDE: Fyris?

DRAFNAR: What does the shield say to that, master ollave?

HERMINTRUDE: The shield?

DRAFNAR: Ay, for I know Feng wrote to Balant that he should kill Hamlet.

OLLAVE: The runes say indeed, ay, that Hamlet took the letter while his companions slept, and, yes, I see, he substituted for it——

DRAFNAR: And this you never knew?

HUGH: Then my master——?

DRAFNAR: Ho, ho, ho, ho!

OLLAVE: This other letter ordered the execution of Cimbal and Carvel?

HUGH: Ay, it ordered their execution.

HERMINTRUDE: Wait. I see in this changing of letters a trick we can play on Balant again—and (*she whispers to the* OLLAVE) on Hamlet. . . .

OLLAVE (*whispers*): Oh——? Aha! (*Then aloud*) Oho! Yes, indeed!

HERMINTRUDE: But go on, Briton.

HUGH: Well, then King Balant received with gratitude a small cargo of amber and made a great feast for the Danes. There were but fifty of them, in a single ship of twenty-three benches, with victuals and ballast. And afterwards I it was—done some service as a spy before I had, small I am, I can insinuate myself. . . .

———

BALANT: Follow them to the house in which they sleep.

HUGH: Indeed, master.

CIMBAL: ⎫
      ⎬ Good night, my lord.
CARVEL: ⎭

BALANT: Good night, gentlemen. And note all.

HUGH: Ay, my lord.

CIMBAL: Good night, my pretty. Or will you rather——?

CARVEL: Sweet dreams, little Cymric maid. Nay, kiss me.

BRITISH VIRGINS: Wild you are, sir. Nay, sir, let her be. There's ungentle. Nay, sir. Oh, sir, leave me.

HAMLET: Good night, sir.

BALANT: Good night, young prince. We shall do all that lies in our power.

HAMLET: I thank you, my lord.

BALANT: Nay, sir. Look, he walks off alone. He took no metheglin and scarcely broke bread.

HUGH: He tasted meat and left it.

BALANT: There is much I do not understand. In this letter, he is praised for his wit, yet his companions openly mock at him. Feng begs me to give him in marriage my daughter Fyris, yet Feng should fear him. As to Carvel, my blood-brother speaks of him as of one of no regard and will have him hanged like a dog with the other. Yet it was Carvel——

HUGH: They return, my lord.

CIMBAL: Again, good night, my lord.

CARVEL: Good night, my lord, again.

BALANT: Good night, gentlemen.

CIMBAL: Our fool has already crept off to bed.

CARVEL: You must forgive him, sir.

BALANT: Nay, gentlemen, it is no doubt my poor hospitality. Or perhaps the sea-voyage. Good night. Good night. Follow them.

HUGH: Ay, master.

BALANT: Then return.

————————

[*A heavy folding door opens, and men are heard snoring.* CIMBAL *and* CARVEL, *shouting, stumble, and* IST CARLE *grunts and wakes.*

CIMBAL: The curse of Frigga light upon you, man.

CARVEL: May you grow impotent. Out of the way.

CIMBAL: Out with flint and steel and make a light for your masters.

CARVEL: Ay.

IST CARLE: Hold on a minute.

CIMBAL: Quicker, man.

CARVEL: Hurry, slave.

IST CARLE: Nay, I'm doing my best. There you are, master.

CIMBAL: Ho, there's the fool Hamlet.

CARVEL: Not yet asleep, fool?

HAMLET: Lie down, and let the men rest.

CARVEL: Nay, sir, we are not pig's meat.

CIMBAL: We are friends of the King.

CARVEL: Of two kings, Feng and Balant.

HAMLET: Much good will it do you. Sodden dogs. Lie down, I say. Here are your blankets.

CARVEL: Listen, all of you. Kick that one, Cimbal. His snoring disturbs me.

[2ND CARLE *grunts and wakes.*

Listen while I tell you how the prince your master——

CIMBAL: *Our* master!

CARVEL: Ay, *our* master!—comports himself at a foreign court.

CIMBAL: Comports himself. . . .

CARVEL: He refuses all meat and mead and sits huddled in silence. The King's daughter, the fair Fyris——

HAMLET: Quiet, man.

CIMBAL: Quiet, man?

HAMLET: I'll play your game. This is why I did not eat or drink. The bread was flecked with blood. There was a tang of iron in the liquor. The meats you feasted on stank of a human carcase. They had a smack of the shambles.

CIMBAL: A smack of the shambles?

CARVEL: What else, fool?

1ST CARLE: You've been to a strange feast, masters.

HAMLET: The British King, moreover, has the eyes of a slave.

CIMBAL: ⎫
⎬ What, fool, what?
CARVEL: ⎭

1ST CARLE: Nay, of a Briton.

HAMLET: And the queen behaved in three ways like a bondmaid.

CIMBAL: O villain, to jeer thus at a king's hospitality and a queen's courtesy.

CARVEL: Now Feng would have no doubt of your wits, unmannerly fool.

1ST CARLE: Nay, master, I fed well enough with the king's carles.

HAMLET: Now go to sleep.

1ST CARLE: Nay, masters, I wish you'd stop arguing about what you've eaten and drunk and let poor folk like me get a bit of sleep.

HAMLET: I said go to sleep. If you can't go to sleep, talk

in whispers. And if you can't talk in whispers, go and hold your flyting-match outside.

———————————

HUGH: . . . And that the queen had exhibited in three respects the deportment of a handmaiden.

BALANT: And that I had the eyes of a slave?

HUGH: Indeed, your majesty, that was the words he uttered.

BALANT: Ay, ay, the man whose tongue speaks such things, either of more than mortal wisdom he is or more than mortal folly. Go, rouse my steward, my baker, the swineherd——

HUGH: I will, your majesty.

BALANT: And stay. Say to the queen mother that I will visit her presently.

HUGH: Ay, sir.

BALANT: And this is he to whom I am to give my daughter!

———————————

BAKER: Indeed, your majesty, true it is. Myself planted that field with grain in the spring, thinking it the more fruitful. And indeed a Roman garrison was massacred there by Frisian pirates, and bones strew the ground in great profusion.

———————————

SWINEHERD: Ay, your majesty, 'twas even so. The hogs strayed from keeping and batten they did on the rotten carcase of a robber, who lay in a ditch.

---

STEWARD: I had men dig deep down in the spring, and there indeed lay swords rusting. The bees too may perhaps have fed in the paunch of a dead man.

---

BALANT: Old witch! I say I'll have the truth out of you by trial.

QUEEN-MOTHER: Nay, then, 'twas so indeed. The king being on service with the Romans, yield myself I did to a slave in his absence, and of this union were you born.

---

BALANT: My lord, why did you not speak of these matters privily to me?

HAMLET: I would have done so. I was angry with my companions.

BALANT: Ay, ay, we know what is to become of them. But tell me, also, in what three respects did my queen demean herself?

HAMLET: It may be that your manners differ from ours, sir. But to a Dane her fashion of muffling her head in her gown, that she gathered up her gown for walking as bondmaids do and that. . . .

BALANT: Nay, speak on.

HAMLET: This picking of her teeth with a splinter, then

chewing up the fragment thus dislodged. She was, I think, a foreign princess, brought into slavery from captivity.

BALANT: I do not marvel, young my lord, that Feng speaks so highly of your judgment. I will put her away. And will you have my daughter Fyris, does she please you?

HAMLET: She does, my lord.

BALANT: A daughter and a grand-daughter of slaves?

HAMLET: She ennobles her birth. And so do you, my lord.

BALANT: It is true, we are all children of Adam.

HAMLET: Of——?

BALANT: Of Odin, my lord. Of Odin, if you will.

HAMLET: I care not, my lord. But I will have your daughter.

———————

BALANT: There, my lord, now all your uncle's commands are fulfilled. The spirits of Cimbal and Carvel, gone they are before the face of the Lord God.

HAMLET: Mm?

BALANT: They have kicked their last.

HAMLET: What? They are hanged?

BALANT: As the King of Jutland's message desired.

HAMLET: The king? The tyrant of Jutland, my usurping uncle, Feng.

FYRIS: Are you not pleased, Amleth?

HAMLET: Ho, they were rogues, but your father cannot hang Danes without a blood-fee.

BALANT: Sir!

HAMLET: Am I to take pleasure in the death of my fellow country-men? Well-born, too. Great thanes.

FYRIS: A blood-fee, my lord?

BALANT: Yes, yes, I know the custom. You shall state the amount, my son.

HAMLET: For king's thanes, let me see, yes, two hundred marks, three——

BALANT: I shall gladly pay it.

HAMLET: Melt down the gold, my lord, and pour it into two hollow sticks.

FYRIS: Two hollow sticks?

[BALANT *laughs.*

HAMLET: You jest, my lord?

BALANT: Nay, sir, that is no Danish custom. I know Latin. I have read Livy. It was a Roman consul in the time of the wicked Tarquin who poured gold into hollow sticks. Brutus, I think—ay, Lucius Junius Brutus.

HAMLET: Then a Dane will for once copy the Romans, my lord.

BALANT: Ah, if I might also bring you to the religion of Rome!

FYRIS: Will you not listen to the word of God in the mouth of my father, Amleth?

HAMLET: I will listen.

FYRIS: And you will not leave me yet, my lord?

BALANT: Ah, no!

HAMLET: I shall return to Jutland next spring. I shall surprise them. My mother has orders to mourn for me a year from my departure. She will prepare a funeral feast, upon which I shall enter. Other matters too will have been prepared by her and by my blood-brother, Drafnar the outlaw.

[HAMLET's *voice is gradually replaced by* HUGH's, *with which it has been synchronised.*

HUGH: . . . That he should return to Jutland in the spring and that he would surprise them. His mother had orders to mourn for him a year after his departure. She was to prepare a funeral feast, upon which he should enter. Other matters too were to have been prepared by her and by his blood-brother, Drafnar, the outlaw.

136

DRAFNAR: Ay, so it was.

HERMINTRUDE: What other matters, Drafnar the out-law?

DRAFNAR: I am well within the law these six weeks, lady.

HERMINTRUDE: What other matters?

DRAFNAR: I was to guard his pointed spits, his mother to weave hangings for the hall.

OLLAVE: Ah, yes, I mind the spits. We recall the spits, my lady, and the hangings, do we not?

HERMINTRUDE: This Fyris?

HUGH: The princess, lady, now the Queen of Jutland. My fair and gentle mistress——

HERMINTRUDE: Enough of her virtues, fellow. Did Hamlet take her to Jutland?

DRAFNAR: Nay, he came back this month to fetch her.

HUGH: Still at her father's court, lady. In Hamlet's absence, she bore his child.

HERMINTRUDE: A daughter?

HUGH: A son.

HERMINTRUDE (*sighs with relief*): Ah!

OLLAVE: You will mind, my lady, what I told you about Danish views on succession. The Britons, too, now that they are Christianised——

HERMINTRUDE: Enough. This tale of the changed letter. You shall tell me, Drafnar, what happened on Hamlet's return to Jutland. But first—you, sirrah.

GODFREY: Great queen.

HERMINTRUDE: My ollave has perchmane, no doubt?

OLLAVE: Very little, my lady, our last consignment——

HERMINTRUDE: Go, the two of you. Ollave, you will brief a letter in this same mingling of ogham with dog Latin, and you, sirrah, will creep back with the same stealth——

OLLAVE: What shall the letter say, great queen?

HERMINTRUDE: Why, coof, that King Balant begs the queen of air and darkness, myself, Hermintrude, to embrace with love this Hamlet, King of Jutland, whose story is told on the shield, and to yield him her hand in marriage.

OLLAVE: My lady!

DRAFNAR: Ho, ho, ho, ho!

HUGH: But the princess?

HERMINTRUDE: Take the shield.

GODFREY: My lady.

HERMINTRUDE: If he still sleeps, place it again beneath his head, and put this dyte where the other lay.

GODFREY: I will, great queen.

DRAFNAR: Hamlet feigned madness and may feign sleep. I doubt whether, while the shield and the letter were taken——

HERMINTRUDE: It matters little enough. Go, the two of you.

OLLAVE:
GODFREY:
} My lady.

HERMINTRUDE: And now, Drafnar, go on.

DRAFNAR: Why, then, Queen Gertrude gave out, at the end of March, that her son was dead. King Feng was happy enough that it should seem so. He too reckoned on grounds of his own that Hamlet was dead. A feast was ordered. I knew that I must be to hand. I could not freely enter the great hall, but Tosti, the dwarf and scald, kept me informed. I stayed about in the yard that night. I rolled away the stone from that hovel in which the pointed stakes were kept. I was ready.

[*The banquet hall in Jutland. The harping and the laughter cease as the doors are flung open.*

HAMLET (*calling from the door*): Good evening to you, uncle.

THE GUESTS: Hamlet! He returns from the dead. Is it his ghost?

HAMLET: I said good evening to you, uncle.

FENG: Good evening, nephew.

GERTRUDE: Hamlet. Oh, my dear Hamlet!

HAMLET (*approaches*): Nay, do not look at me as if I were dead. I live. Though I am still light in the head, as you see. Is there no place for me to sit and eat?

GERTRUDE: Sit here by me, Hamlet.

FENG: A place for the lord Hamlet!

HAMLET: I'll join the cup-bearers. Come, give me a great ewer. Here! Here, I say!

STEWARD: Ay, my lord.

HAMLET: Here, uncle, let me fill up this horn again. You gave my father horns——

GERTRUDE: Hamlet!

HAMLET: —it is fitting I should——

FENG: Steady, Hamlet, steady.

[HAMLET *spills the liquor over* FENG. *From everybody, relieved laughter.*

FENG: Nay, look, man. I see that roving has not mended your wits.

HAMLET: Who else is thirsty?

GUESTS: Here, here, Hamlet.

[HAMLET *goes among the guests, singing.*

HAMLET: Old King Cole of Norway
Came to Jutland's strand,
He set his lean white horses
Nibbling away at the land.

Horwendill with a sunny brow
Met him in a March dawn,
Hewed his foot off under the bough,
Red on a frosted lawn.

Sela now the wintry moon
He picked out of the sky,
Warmed sweet Groa's lith by noon
And filled her womb with a sigh.

FENG: And yet he must be watched. Gertrude, you
swore he was dead. And indeed I believed it. Where are
his companions, Cimbal and Carvel?

HAMLET: This was the summer of Orwendel,
He reigned a year and no more,
Two grey axes silently fell
Either side of his door.

Earth lies locked in winter's embrace
Again, but not for long
Till the fool of the spring with his ashen face
Is heard in a midnight song.

141

DRAFNAR: Hamlet had changed his regal garments, snapped his garters and once more smeared his face with filth. And yet he was changed. He was leaner, more like a man. When he was asked concerning Cimbal and Carvel, he showed them his two hollow sticks, saying that here were both the one and the other. As he plied with the cup-bearers, to prevent his loose dress hampering his walk, he girt his sword tightly over his cloak. He drew it once or twice and purposely pricked his finger with the point. Seeing this, Feng had his attendants rivet both sword and scabbard together with a nail, so that he could not draw it (you will see why). In time, the queen and all her ladies left the hall. Then Hamlet poured out draught upon draught of liquor, till the lords were so deep drenched and their limbs so feeble they began to slide beneath the ale-benches asleep.

TOSTI: Odin wanders    in thorpe and thwaite,
carle and carline    encounter him
by beck and brig,    where the brock cowers,
old and bowed    with a bent rick.

[*He goes on plucking the harp, without declamation.* HAMLET
*is at the door. There is a great noise of drunken singing,
mingled with yawns and snores.*

HAMLET: Are you there, blood-brother?

DRAFNAR: I am here, Hamlet.

HAMLET: Are they ripe, do you think?

DRAFNAR: Here are the spit-faggots.

142

HAMLET: Go, pile brushwood about the house.

DRAFNAR: You will——?

HAMLET: Ay, in a while. First I must pull down my mother's hangings and peg them all to the ground. My mother is gone to bed. I'll get Tosti to——

DRAFNAR: Here comes the king.

HAMLET: Good night, my lord. I have but now opened the door for you.

FENG (*thickly*): Good night, Hamlet. I am happy to see you. Happy to see you. Roving, I see, has not mended your wits. Roving, I see, has—— (*Exit.*)

HAMLET: Nor will it mend yours, uncle. To the wood-pile then, Drafnar.

DRAFNAR: Ay, we'll light all Jutland.

[HAMLET *goes back into the hall. There are now more snores and yawns than singing.*

HAMLET: Leave your harp, Tosti.

TOSTI: Ah, my dear lord!

HAMLET: From this night on, you shall sing a more honest song, Tosti. Leave the merry wood and help me pull down these hangings upon the sleepers.

TOSTI: With joy, my lord!

HAMLET: Peg them together with these.

[*He throws down the faggots. Together they tear down the hangings and tangle them about the sleepers.*

HAMLET: I think you did not love my father. Here!

TOSTI: You spat in my face and told Feng when I sang the Orwendill song. Now spit!

HAMLET: Quickly, or they'll choke before we can burn them.

TOSTI: What of the king, my lord?

HAMLET: Wait, Tosti. Ah, there, that has you fast, my lord. Ay, Tosti. I'll save the best dish till the end.

TOSTI: Ah, how long have I waited for this night to come. There, there, and a kick from my lame foot!

HAMLET: Come now to the door. Drafnar!

DRAFNAR: Ay, my lord. It is done.

HAMLET: A torch, then. There, bar the door. The window slits will do for a draught.

[*They fire the brushwood.*

HAMLET: Good night, rabble of Jutland. Now to the king.

DRAFNAR: Shall I——?

TOSTI: My lord?

HAMLET: I'll to the king alone.

———————

HAMLET: Awake, my lord. The house is on fire.

GERTRUDE: Hamlet, what is it?

HAMLET: Mother, go.

GERTRUDE: Hamlet——

HAMLET: Say nothing, go.

FENG: Gertrude!

HAMLET: Now I'll change swords. Yours, uncle, is now riveted by your own decree.

FENG: What, what . . .? Hamlet!

HAMLET: I come to slay you, uncle.

FENG: Hamlet! What further madness is this?

HAMLET: Look, uncle. That is your great hall burning. I shall need a great hall when I am king, but I will not have one polluted by you.

FENG: My sword, my sword. Ah!

HAMLET: Besides, there are some dozens of your friends in there I thought fit to roast. Cimbal and Carvel died a year ago. Carvel, I think, helped you kill my father? There, uncle, steady. Did you not have it nailed into the scabbard, lest I prick my fingers?

FENG: What?

HAMLET: I changed swords. Stand back, uncle. Give the executioner room. Nay, flail not so with a blunt scabbard. Ha? Well, then, a flailing match, but my flail has an edge. There! I missed you, uncle. Your neck, then. There! Ah, his shoulder. Now the neck. Again, there!

[*The music takes up* FENG'S *scream and hovers.*

HAMLET: Forgive my first clumsiness, uncle. And now, dead sir—parricide, lecher—I'll trouble you for your head. With this, old blubber-lips, I'll make your people laugh, my people, that you have made weep so long. For they who laughed while you lived are by now ash.

[*A great crackling, splitting timbers.*

HAMLET: Ay, ay, the roof of Feng's great hall falls.

[*It does, mightily.*

HAMLET: And all this shall be painted on a shield.

———————

HERMINTRUDE: Where are those we sent out?

OLLAVE: Ay, the scurriors?

DRAFNAR: Shall I guess?

HERMINTRUDE: Did you frame the new letter as I bade you?

OLLAVE: In the smallest particular, great queen. In rude ogham and very bad Latin, with a dash of Cymric.

146

HERMINTRUDE: Then they will come, with sword sheathed.

DRAFNAR: And a red shield, lady, for with us blood-colour means peace.

HERMINTRUDE: As for you, fellow——

HUGH (*nervously*): Your majesty!

HERMINTRUDE: We thank you for your tale.

HUGH: My lady, King Balant, my master——

HERMINTRUDE: Think not on him. You remain with us until this tale is done, and the red shield stands or a battle is added to the other. Meanwhile, Drafnar-within-the-law, tell us how the rest of that night turned out and what happened on the morrow.

OLLAVE: Ay, how did the people take it?

DRAFNAR: Why, then, when Hamlet bade the queen leave the bride-bower, I kept her with me till the prince came out, holding Feng's head by the hairs. Afterwards, the queen would not stay in that place, but we together went to the hovel in which Hamlet had kept his pointed stakes. The burning of the hall had not passed un-marked, but the few carles and carlines who left their homes to see what it was, Hamlet or the queen bade go back till morning. Then, from every house and farmstead in that part of Jutland, jarl and carle came riding together, to see what beacon had all night reddened the sky. There was no tumult. Each man feared his neigh-bour, for some were friends of Feng, and others remem-bered Orwendill.

———————

3RD CARLE: Looker at all t charred bodies ligging i t ruins o th house.

2ND CARLE: Ay, we mun wend. Feng's done this in his rage.

1ST CARLE: Nay, they were Feng's mates.

4TH CARLE: Feng's ligging here hissen, bout head.

CARLES: Eh?

[*A carline screams.*

1ST CARLE: Who's done this?

2ND CARLE: Did they raid t coast fro Norway?

3RD CARLE: Wa they Goths or Easterlings?

4TH CARLE: They reckon mad Amleth's back.

3RD CARLE: Is he? Thou sailed wi Amleth.

1ST CARLE: Ay, he's back.

2ND CARLE: Happen we'd best go arm ussens.

3RD CARLE: There'll be hummer to play.

CARLINE: Int there none on you boun to look for t murderer?

4TH CARLE: I'm fleyed.

1st CARLE: Ay, best keep quiet and bide.

2nd CARLE: Feng's been no use to folk like me. It were him killed Orwendill.

3rd CARLE: Nobdy'll miss this lot.

CARLINE: Yonder's t queen. And mad Amleth.

2nd CARLE: He's gate Drafnar with him an all.

3rd CARLE: Yon's dwarf Tosti still hopping, choose how.

1st CARLE: I reckon it were Amleth gate shut o Cimbal and Carvel.

CARLINE: Long live t queen.

4th CARLE: Long live t queen.

[*They all cry*, "Long live Queen Groa."

GERTRUDE: People of Jutland. . . .

CARLES: Quiet. Harken to t queen. They're boun to speak.

GERTRUDE: People of Jutland, give ear to my son, now your liege, the prince Hamlet.

CARLES: He's recovered his wits, then? Yon dateless fooil! He neer wa mad, I reckon. Nay, let's hear em.

HAMLET: If there be any among you, thanes of Denmark and good people of Jutland, that as yet hold fresh within your memories the wrong done to my father, be not moved by this sight. Behold the body not of a king but of a parricide. It was a worse thing to see when the body of Orwendill lay butchered under his own eaves. Remember——

CARLES: This is no dateless fooil. He's reight enow. Feng wa no use.

HAMLET: Remember how kindly Orwendill fostered you, how justly dealt with you, how dearly loved you. The hand that slew this good king made you slaves. Your rights were forfeited, the yoke planted on your necks. Plagues overran us. The sea ate away the land. All this is over now. Here is one justly punished, caught in his own toils, the killer of his kin. As to the doer of this deed, he stands here before you. I, Hamlet, son of Orwendill, grandson of the high king and rightful heir to the seat of Jutland. You know the story of my wrongs, how in childhood, to escape the wrath of Feng and the same death as my father, I put on madness, while this butcher sported in my mother's arms. . . .

GERTRUDE: Hamlet!

HAMLET: Nay, mother, your infamy is quenched. Your queen repented the night I killed Hunferth, the high king's counsellor, and has since nursed with me this just revenge. Many of you, loathing Feng, would have helped me to this deed. I needed only Drafnar, my sworn brother, whom Feng outlawed for his loyalty, and this faithful dwarf, Tosti the saga-teller. I wished to do this deed alone. Feng's helpers I have burnt. His own trunk lies here, headless. On this at least you may wreak your loathing, you whose sons, fathers, wives, land, he took. Now pile up the pyre. Burn the evil man's body, consume away his guilty limbs, scatter his sinful ashes, strew broadcast his pitiless dust. Let no urn or barrow house him. Let there be no place in his own land marked with his name. Let no vicinity suck infection from his carcase, neither sea nor soil be defiled by harbouring these accursed bones. And pay now the homage that you owe. I have wiped off my country's shame. I have stripped you of slavery and clothed you with freedom. In your hands is the reward. I sue for my wages.

1ST CARLE: I sailed wi thee, Amleth. Thou has my voice.

2ND CARLE: Long live King Amleth!

CARLES AND CARLINES: Long live King Amleth!

HAMLET: And what say the earls and thanes?

1ST EARL: I yield you fealty, son of Orwendill.

2ND EARL: And I.

3RD EARL: And I. Long live King Hamlet.

ALL: Long live King Amleth! Long live t new king! Reign Amleth in Jutland! We will serve thee, Hamlet, son of Orwendill.

———

DRAFNAR: And the end of it was they made him king. A month later we sailed for Britain to fetch his bride, Fyris.

OLLAVE: Ah, a brave and a gash——

151

HERMINTRUDE: There is one thing in this story which does not please me, and that is Fyris.

[*Enter* GODFREY, *dishevelled*.

GODFREY: Great queen——

HERMINTRUDE: Well?

GODFREY: They are coming to the palace. They relaxit me to run ahead.

OLLAVE: } They——?

HERMINTRUDE: }

[DRAFNAR *roars with laughter*.

GODFREY: My lady, I bent to place the shield beneath the young king's head and to put the new screed in his coffer. He rose suddenly from his feigned sleep and seized me by the arms.

HERMINTRUDE: Has he read——?

GODFREY: I canna tell, my lady.

OLLAVE: I hear their horses.

HERMINTRUDE: Am I beautiful, Drafnar?

DRAFNAR: Lady, I——

HERMINTRUDE: More beautiful than Fyris, Briton?

HUGH: Queen, I——

HERMINTRUDE: My lord of tongues?

OLLAVE: White queen of birth and infancy, red brichit of love and battle, wan sibyl of death and divination, we adore thee in the morrow of the bean-flower and the hawthorn, the high noon of the poppy and the rowan-berry, the night of the sloe and the winter heliotrope.

[*Enter* GUARDS.

GUARDS: The Danes are here, great queen.

[*Enter* HAMLET *and his retinue.* HAMLET *stands apart.*

DANISH CAPTAINS: We greet you, Queen of Picts.

HERMINTRUDE: And which of you all is Hamlet?

HAMLET: I am the King of Jutland, my lady.

HERMINTRUDE: We have heard your story, king.

HAMLET: Did it please you, lady?

HERMINTRUDE: Greatly. Approach, my lord, if you please, and sit here on this empty throne beside us.

HAMLET: My lady.

HERMINTRUDE: We have been told, young Jutland, that you bear messages from aged Britain.

HAMLET: Here is his tablet.

HERMINTRUDE: Read it, ollave. But sit, my lord.

HAMLET: I will. I thank you.

OLLAVE: "We, Balant, king of north-east Cumbria, do request of our neighbour and peer, Queen Hermintrude of the Picts, Cathbregion and Brithwyr in Manau Gododin, that she make welcome the young King of Jutland, grandson of the high King Roderick of Denmark, and that she be pleased to bestow upon this prince her royal and most lovely hand——"

HAMLET (*hypocritical*): Mm?

OLLAVE: "—in token whereof——"

HAMLET: This is strange.

HERMINTRUDE: It does not please you, my lord?

HAMLET: My father-in-law is a man of Christian humility, lady. It is clear that, as he sees these things, his own daughter barely suffices me for a bride. Or perhaps her recent motherhood suggests to him that——

HERMINTRUDE: My, lord, we are said abroad to behave with grim cruelty to those who look for our favours. It may be that Balant sought your death——

HAMLET: My death?

DRAFNAR: Did you know that Feng and the King of Britain had sworn blood-brotherhood, Hamlet?

HAMLET: Did I? No, I think not.

HERMINTRUDE: There is something slavish about this King of Britain.

HAMLET: His father was a slave.

HERMINTRUDE: Are you content, my lord, to be mated to a slave's grandchild?

HAMLET: I had been content.

HERMINTRUDE: And to pour into your son's veins the blood of slaves?

HAMLET: I am less content at that.

HERMINTRUDE: My lord, am I beautiful?

[A pause.

HAMLET: You are beautiful, Queen Hermintrude.

HERMINTRUDE: And I am not a slave, Hamlet. Between my coast and Jutland, nothing intervenes. My people need amber.

HAMLET: They shall have it, lady.

HERMINTRUDE: I yield my kingdom with myself, my sceptre and my hand together.

[A pause.

HERMINTRUDE: Well, my lord?

HAMLET: With how many men can I go to fetch my first bride and my child?

HERMINTRUDE: With enough to fight if Balant wishes.

HAMLET: I will marry you.

HERMINTRUDE: Ah. . . .

––––––––––––––

DRAFNAR: What is that in front?

HAMLET: Where?

TOSTI: I see a cloud of dust.

HAMLET: British dust?

TOSTI: Little enough of it.

HAMLET: Call a halt.

DRAFNAR: Halt! Halt!

CAPTAIN 1: Halt!

CAPTAIN 2: Halt!

HAMLET: Now what do your poet's eyes see?

TOSTI: The King of Britain's daughter with twelve retainers.

HAMLET: Fyris?

DRAFNAR: There are not more than twelve.

HAMLET: Let us ride a little way ahead.

DRAFNAR: Has her father driven her out of doors, or has she fled?

FYRIS (*distant*): Amleth! Amleth!

TOSTI: She seems in some agitation.

HAMLET: Hm.

FYRIS: Amleth!

DRAFNAR: Take care, Hamlet. Twelve Britons have twelve swords.

HAMLET: Mere weight of metal. Draw rein.

FYRIS: Amleth! Amleth, my dear love!

HAMLET: What is it, Fyris, my wife?

FYRIS: Ah, once your wife, Amleth!

HAMLET: So——?

FYRIS: I do not wish to speak of your——

HAMLET: My——?

FYRIS: Perhaps the laws of the Picts are different, Amleth. I would suppose her your paramour. But unworthy I should think it of myself to hate you more as an adulterer than love you as a husband.

HAMLET: Fyris, I——

FYRIS: I do not shrink from you, my lord! No. I am come to tell you what is intended against you by my father.

HAMLET: Ha?

FYRIS: A son I have as a pledge of our marriage, and regard for him, if nothing else, must incline me, his mother, to the affection of a wife. The time will come when he may hate the queen who usurped his mother's place, but I will love her. No calamity shall quench my flame for you, no malice put it out nor stay me from laying before you——

HAMLET: Come, then.

FYRIS: No kindness? Well, then, beware of your father-in-law, Hamlet. His ambassador has stolen his prize, and——

HAMLET: He intended my death at the queen's hand.

FYRIS: No, Amleth!

HAMLET: What else?

FYRIS: My lord, it is not easy or pleasant for me to betray my father.

DRAFNAR: Hamlet——

TOSTI: There is another cloud of dust. This time it is larger.

DRAFNAR: This is Balant.

TOSTI: There is no king with them, but they are Balant's men.

HAMLET: Yes. . . . (*With a beginning of tenderness*) Fyris, my wife, I . . . (*He sighs.*) How many are there?

DRAFNAR: Twenty or thirty.

HAMLET: So they do not come to fight?

DRAFNAR: Perhaps not——

FYRIS: No. They are told to welcome you, Amleth. You are to be greeted with a banquet. But under the porch of the folding doors you——

HAMLET: Ah, so was my father slain. I will put on a shirt of little rings. Is our son well?

FYRIS: He is well, my lord.

HAMLET: Drafnar——

DRAFNAR: My lord.

HAMLET: Back to the main body and tell off two hundred horse to follow two hundred yards behind.

DRAFNAR (*joyously*): I will, my lord.

HAMLET: Wait. The spy who took away my shield will ride with me. He shall persuade Balant that in all this I am blameless.

———————

HAMLET (*hurt*): Ah . . .!

BALANT: So, defiler of my daughter, polluter of my kingdom, Feng's regicide——

159

HAMLET: Nay, father-in-law, you have not slain me yet. But the point of your javelin is between these steel rings.

BALANT: So——?

HAMLET: Your daughter warned me, old fool. Now listen——

GODFREY: It is true, O Balant, I stole your letter while the young King of Jutland slept, and the court ollave changed its purport.

HAMLET: Would you have an ambassador read the letter he bears?

BALANT: I think there was some story of a changed inscription before, heathen dog.

HAMLET: Before?

BALANT: Where is my daughter, infidel? Ho, there, *comites*!

HAMLET: You rage, old fool. Your daughter is in the Pictish camp.

BALANT: Ho, there! Ah, but I will fetch her to-morrow. Ho, I say!

GODFREY: His guards, my lord.

HAMLET: I will hang you the day after, father-in-law. To-morrow, in chains, you shall see your daughter and your grandson for the last time, with my new queen. After that, three kingdoms, not two, shall be one beneath a Danish king. For the moment, I spare your old bones.

[BALANT's *guards*, *approaching*, *shout* "Which way, My Lord?"

BALANT: Ho, there, *gosgordd*!

GODFREY: Come, my lords. He will bid them slay us. Our horses have wandered off and are over there feeding on a bank.

BALANT: Ho, there, I say! I will make an end of two heathen kingdoms at once. God shall prevail in me.

HAMLET: Roman slave! This is the end of peace for Britain. I will join the Jutes in the south and crack you like a nut.

---

MINIMUS: Good morning, gentlemen.

OLLAVE: Good morrow to you.

MINIMUS: A fair day it is.

OLLAVE: Ay, the laverock's i the lift. It soars aboon the haugh and the green bear. The mavis and the lintwhite, the cushat and the gowk——

TOSTI: Who is this?

OLLAVE: Eh? Oh, the British bard. Minimus, I believe?

MINIMUS: Ay, man. King Balant's master-poet. *Vox poetica sempervivet.*

OLLAVE: Latin. Mind, I've heard scholarship contend that your ain runes are howkit frae——

TOSTI: Ah!

MINIMUS: Hey!

OLLAVE: What are you up to, man?

TOSTI: A traitor, a Briton, here? Why, slay him, lessen the accursed breed by one.

OLLAVE: A wee scrimpet billy like him, too. Tosti, man, sheathe your whittle.

TOSTI: Then you, Pict, are in league with the enemy, a traitor, a spy?

OLLAVE: Tell me, friend, what is a poet?

TOSTI: I, sir, am a Dane.

OLLAVE: They told me you were a poet, a saga-teller— what do they call you?—a scald.

TOSTI: I am a Danish poet.

MINIMUS: What college you were at, sir?

OLLAVE: Look, my friend, Britons are but Roman slaves, living like rabbits amid the ruined stone houses of their late masters, but——

MINIMUS: Picts, sir, are hag-ridden gipsies who paint their faces and copulate in public like dogs. Nevertheless——

162

OLLAVE: Natheless, sir, a poet is a poet——

MINIMUS: The *pencerdd* enjoys a privilege superior to that of a mere *civitas* or nation——

OLLAVE: And in these two kingdoms, when a battle is fought, the bards of both sides meet cummerlike at the most conveniable point of vantage and join battle in crambo-clink.

MINIMUS: Ay, indeed. *Non amici, fratres, non sanguine, corde.*

OLLAVE: So we'll employ neither dirk nor gully.

[*A pause.*

TOSTI: Gentlemen, forgive me. This is a good law, which is not understood in Jutland, nor anywhere in Denmark, Norway or among the Easterlings. I do not know what my companions will think of me, but it is a good law.

MINIMUS: Hm.

OLLAVE: Ye maun credit him, my friend. Nor maun ye despise his lear. Gin these Teutonic peoples are no far-seen in Latin or Greek, this scald may yet bear the gree and pat us both to shame. I hae listed to some o their saga-telling. 'Tis nae sheep-shank. It alliterates excessively, like your own *cynghanedd*, but——

MINIMUS: What do you say, man?

OLLAVE: Nor do they well ken that a poem is aye a conjuration of the triune goddess——

MINIMUS: Ah, things are changed in Britain nowadays.

OLLAVE: You mean the Christian doctrine?

MINIMUS: Ay, ay, ay. Now we have a triune fish-and-father god instead. We may not invoke Rhiannon openly except as the mother of this new God, as Mary, eternally virgin.

OLLAVE: A fish god with a virgin mother?

MINIMUS: To make the idea of patrilineal succession doubly plain.

OLLAVE: Is it so?

MINIMUS: Instead of the birth and death of the seasons, we are made to celebrate the liturgical year. Annwn is with Llyn Llion, drowned. Llyr is dead. Lleu is dead too. Lludd, Nudd and Hu.

OLLAVE: But not Aeron?

MINIMUS: Eh?

[*From the plain we hear the assembly of armies.*

TOSTI: Ah, they come.

OLLAVE: Ay, touts the trumpet. The swankies a foregather, ram-stam and throuther, tapsalteery for the brattle. We three maun link tae our work.

[*They tune their harps.*

164

MINIMUS: Will you inaugurate the proceedings, sir?

OLLAVE: Ay, do.

[TOSTI *clears his throat and plucks the harp.*

TOSTI: Shout, spear-Dane sons   of Shield Sheafing, . . .

MINIMUS:
OLLAVE: } Very good, very good.

TOSTI: . . . foam-neck farers.   Kit flashes.

MINIMUS: Kit?

OLLAVE: A sword, a *gladium*.

MINIMUS: Ah!

TOSTI: Gold gleamed   the gannet's bath, . . .

MINIMUS: Gannet's——?

OLLAVE: One of their commoner kennings for the sea.

MINIMUS: Indeed?

TOSTI: . . . bearing blond fighters   to blood's acre.

OLLAVE:
MINIMUS: } Ah!

TOSTI: Now swells the heart    of the swart Briton,
all unheeding    the guile of Hamlet.
The eagle and crow    confer together,
the wan wolf    now leaves his woodland.
All are eager.    Their eyes narrow . . .

---

BALANT: Holy, holy, holy! Lord God of Battles, look
down upon the children of thy grace assembled before
thee in earthly Sion.

BRITONS: Amen.

BALANT: Fall they shall to-day upon the New Babylon
and utterly cast down that place of abomination in thy
sight.

BRITONS: Amen.

BALANT: Lord God of Jacob, Isaac and Abraham——

BRITONS: Lord God of Jacob, Isaac and Abraham——

BALANT: Hold up these sons of thy mercy with the
strength of thy right arm. Stand before them like a shield
of triple brass.

BRITONS: Praise the Lord.

BALANT: We fight to-day against the unbaptised and the
uncircumcised——

BRITONS: Emmanuel.

BALANT: —the heathen and the howling fiend of hell.
The mark of the beast is upon him. The smoke of his

torment shall rise up from generation unto generation. But to-day——

BRITONS: Emmanuel. God with us.

BALANT: Ye that have fought the Picts before, ye know them, whited sepulchres, cowardice and corruption within. But many among you knock for the first time upon those white ox-hide shields, those countenances caked with chalk and gypsum, those blue-ringed eyes. Nay, ye shall thrust against women——

BRITONS: Oh!

BALANT: —Jezebel in arms, tilting against you with javelins——

BRITONS: Oh! Oh!

BALANT: —fornicators and cannibals. Ah, little St. Ninian could do among these eaters of their own kind or Patrick among the bestial Irish. Remember, too, the abominable heresies of Pelagius.

BRITONS: Oh!

BALANT: And the Danes are worse, offerers of burnt sacrifice, bigamists who slay their uncles.

BRITONS: Oh!

BALANT: Strike them down in the name of the Lord of Hosts. Lay them low. Fall not into the defilement of their hands.

BRITONS: Allelujah!

167

BALANT: Ay, that is the cry Germanus taught us. For us, no other cry of battle all this day. Allelujah!

BRITONS: Allelujah!

BALANT: Those that die we shall view with envy, that before us they sail into the bliss of heavenly Sion, their souls wafted. . . .

----

HAMLET: Our foes are many, our friends of doubtful heart. But the meanest of Danish house-carles is not taken into service unless he will face four men without going back. These Cymry are slothful, treacherous, of short stature and full of religion. Men of Jutland, fight well. This horde will break itself upon us, and at home in Jutland . . .

----

HERMINTRUDE: *Cruithneach!* I behold before me not a sea, but a little mountain lake of white shields and blue-ringed eyes. Natheless, as ye worship the goddess, this pool shall teem and its progeny flow upon the whole land in spate. Numbers I despise. They are the calculations of old men, laying pebble to pebble in a line. The goddess is a broch, a tall fort of vitrified stone. They shall stand spell-bound by her pitiless eye and rest in foolishness under the green sod. The dove shall tear down the eagle out of the sky.

PICTS: The cushat shall possess the eyrie.

HERMINTRUDE: Fight well. The cauldron of the triune goddess simmers on the red coals of battle and desire. . . .

----

BALANT: *Gwyr y Gogledd*, sit well your mounts and rush on swift feet.

BRITONS: *Cymru am byth!*

BALANT: I give you the order. Forward, in the name of the Lord!

BRITISH CHIEFS: Forward! Forward! Forward! Forward!

BRITONS: Allelujah! Allelujah! Allelujah! Allelujah!

---

[*The three poets are declaiming simultaneously to their harps.*

OLLAVE: The Cruithneach labour in a void of silence.
   They stagger.
The oxhide shields fall,
Their hands numb.

TOSTI: The rings of the singing sark
Shatter, split.
The crow waits for the waverer.
Eagles yelp.

MINIMUS: Cumbria forms her battle-line.
There in far wood
They run forward,
Their own fair word,
"Allelujah!" cry and the name of the true God.
Danes and Picts turn and fly,
The heathen host.

OLLAVE: Och, hold your whist, man!

TOSTI: Enough, fellow!

MINIMUS: Blows fall,
Bliss fails.

TOSTI: Quiet, you slavish rascal.

OLLAVE: The battle's over, haverel sam.

MINIMUS: Wolf hid in forest
Will feed on fairest.

OLLAVE: Come, we'll leave him.

TOSTI: Let him stay croaking to himself.

MINIMUS: They are trodden into the sod by hooves of
Christ.
Cymry alone stand on the field.
Turn, Beelzebub, and yield!
*Gwyddyl Ffichti*, Brithwyr,
Cannibal whores, spawn of Ercwlf. . . .

------

HERMINTRUDE: So this is how the Jutlanders lead men
into battle? You were not raiding a harmless village,
Hamlet.

HAMLET: There is another day to-morrow. To-morrow
we re-form and fight again.

FYRIS: Oh, Amleth, why do you not make peace with
my father? I will ride to him this very night; to-morrow
you shall embrace.

GODFREY: A hundred Danes were fighting a hundred
duels. They paid no attention to the main body.

OLLAVE: What we need is pipers. Send back for a band of pipers, my lady. How can men fight out of the sound of the pibroch?

DRAFNAR: I tell you, these Picts keep no order. They are like sheep on the hills. They broke at the first onset.

HAMLET: Yet where are the men who will fight to-morrow? They cut down half my army.

OLLAVE: What we require is pipers, my lady. The blood of a Pict calls for the skirl of the pibroch to chill it, or it runs too hot.

GODFREY: Shall I bid them send pipers with the reinforcements, great queen?

HERMINTRUDE: Ay, if pipers will inflate your courage.

DRAFNAR: Can reinforcements be there in time?

OLLAVE: Ay, the twain'll twin and twine——

HERMINTRUDE: Twin and——?

OLLAVE: Nae pact wi the Pict, blethers Balant——

HERMINTRUDE: Pict? Pact?

OLLAVE: Yet gin the people hear a peep o the pipes, ablins this herpler, this pupil o the pope, wi his yeld beld pow purple and his papal hallelujah, he'll allow you——

HERMINTRUDE: Fellow!

171

DRAFNAR: Your queen is speaking to you.

GODFREY: Pst, the queen, man!

TOSTI: Can't you hear?

HERMINTRUDE: What alliterative madness is this?

OLLAVE: I got carried away, my lady. It comes o consorting wi scalds and *cynghogion*-coiners, wi——

HERMINTRUDE: To be accounted mad among these people, a man would need to speak plain sense.

OLLAVE: 'Tis so, 'tis so. The P-Celts are the worst.

[*Enter two* CARLES.

1ST CARLE: My lord!

2ND CARLE: Lord Amleth!

HERMINTRUDE: What is this?

DRAFNAR: What news from Jutland?

1ST CARLE: ⎫
⎬ My lord——
2ND CARLE: ⎭

HAMLET: Well?

1ST CARLE: We've nobbut just beached.

2ND CARLE: Ay.

HAMLET: And——?

1ST CARLE: Th high king——

2ND CARLE: Roderick's deed, my lord.

DRAFNAR: So?

HAMLET: Who reigns in Denmark?

1ST CARLE: Wiglek, my lord.

HAMLET:
DRAFNAR: } Wiglek!
TOSTI:

2ND CARLE: Ay.

FYRIS: Is it ill news, my lord?

HERMINTRUDE: So the King of Jutland has a new master?

HAMLET: Roderick's son. Again, an uncle.

1ST CARLE: T queen-mother towd us to come to you, my lord.

2ND CARLE: Your foster-sister——

HAMLET: Ay, what of Thora?

1ST CARLE: Wiglek's come fro Zealand, my lord.

2ND CARLE: Fjalar an all.

HAMLET: Ah!

DRAFNAR: Fjalar!

TOSTI: A knave!

1ST CARLE: And Fjalar——

HAMLET: Well?

1ST CARLE: He's t gaffer i Scania.

2ND CARLE: Ay.

HAMLET: Fjalar now rules in Scania? And what does Wiglek intend with him in Jutland?

HERMINTRUDE: What does this mean, Hamlet? Is Fjalar to be your overlord?

FYRIS: Amleth, make peace with my father, and let us all join together against your uncle.

OLLAVE: The woes of Pictland are waxing. O Cruith-neach, bow your heads before the doom that is to come.

DRAFNAR: Fjalar's a knave, as Tosti says. And I think Wiglek favoured Feng in the quarrel with Orwendill.

TOSTI: He will pester your mother with all manner of insolence, Hamlet.

GODFREY: I will go. To-morrow's battle shall be ours. And I will bring pipers.

———————

WIGLEK: Silence!

FJALAR: Silence!

GERTRUDE: Be still, my bower-maidens. The high king wishes to speak with us alone. Go your ways.

WIGLEK: And this girl?

GERTRUDE: My foster-child. She remains here, brother. You also have your servant——

FJALAR: Ha?

WIGLEK: Your overlord, Gertrude.

GERTRUDE: My son is my overlord, freely elected by the people and thanes of Jutland.

WIGLEK: Jutland is a province. I am High King of Denmark——

GERTRUDE: More's the pity, brother.

WIGLEK: —and therefore of Jutland. Your son treacherously hacked down the rightful king appointed by my father and yours to be Orwendill's successor——

GERTRUDE: And by you to be his murderer?

FJALAR: Orwendill was a freebooter.

175

WIGLEK: So is his son. Denmark is a kingdom. I will not have governors of provinces leave their people to fare on pirate raids.

GERTRUDE: King Hamlet has gone to fetch his wife.

FJALAR: His wives.

WIGLEK: Ay, his wives. Did you know, Gertrude, that he is now mated with a vampire queen of Pictland?

GERTRUDE: Since when is a King of Jutland forbidden to marry twice?

WIGLEK: Since I established this kingdom.

FJALAR: And we are now at war with Britain.

GERTRUDE: What, putting down some Roman slave?

WIGLEK: With Balant, my lady. Your late husband's blood-brother.

GERTRUDE: What, he and Feng were sworn?

WIGLEK: Ay, Balant must slay his own son-in-law.

THORA: If he can.

FJALAR: The better if he does.

WIGLEK: He will. What can a few Picts do? If he lives, he pays tribute to me, sister, and bows the knee to Fjalar, as you do meanwhile. Come, Fjalar.

GERTRUDE: Ah, God of battles, be with my son.

THORA: Freya be with him, goddess of his love and mine.

WIGLEK: Come, leave the women to wail.

FJALAR: They have cause.

GERTRUDE: Bring the bower-maidens to us, again.

THORA: Ho, virgins of the bride-bower!

GERTRUDE: What battle is toward to-day? How fares my son?

THORA: How fares the king whose first but not last lover I was? Ho, maids of the bride-bower, come back to the queen.

GERTRUDE: Come back, my son, while this Fjalar's greed is still bounded.

1ST BOWER-MAIDEN: What's the matter, my lady?

2ND BOWER-MAIDEN: What does Wiglek want, my lady?

3RD BOWER-MAIDEN: Why is Fjalar with him, my lady?

GERTRUDE: What takes place this day upon a field of blood in Dalriada or Bernicia?

------

HAMLET: Come, tie them to these posts. Prop them kneeling against rocks.

DRAFNAR: Break their knees if they will not.

HAMLET: Tie them to the pommel. Thrust their dead feet into stirrups.

TOSTI: Ay, they are rigid enough in death. But their chins are not set like a warrior's bent on battle.

GODFREY: This is a brave device, setting the dead to fight.

HAMLET: It is near dawn. Drive off the crows. These men will have no eyes to see the foe.

DRAFNAR: Away, black scavengers. They are like Christians.

TOSTI: They sing like British poets. This is a brave *englyn*. Nay, they will settle again.

1ST CARLE: Nay, Dan lad, don't glare at me that road. All I'm doing is extending thy fighting days. All thy wounds is i t front, lad, none i t rick. Thou're in Valhalla, I know, but thy corpse can lend us a hand to-day.

2ND CARLE: Nay, Erik lad, I'll mark thee. Then happen it'll be Valhalla for thee an all.

DRAFNAR: These Picts keep better order dead. Up, guts, there. Face to the foe. There's granite at your back.

———————

BALANT: Soldiers of baptism——

BRITONS: Sela!

BALANT: —yesterday, we halved the infidel host. To-day there shall not live a heathen in North Britain—devils, distillers.

BRITONS: Woe to the children of Erof.

BALANT: To horse, equestrian knights. Foot-soldiers, lift up your consecrated arms. Now death to the infidel——

BRITONS: Death!

BALANT: —death to the adulterer——

BRITONS: Death!

BALANT: —death to the *Gwyddyl Ffichti* and the ravening harlot!

BRITONS: Emmanuel! God with us! Praise the Lord!

——————————

MINIMUS: Good morning, gentlemen.

OLLAVE: Good morning to you, sir.

TOSTI: Good day, sir.

MINIMUS: I greatly admire the obstinacy of the Danes and Picts, gentlemen.

OLLAVE: ⎫
⎬ Ah, yes.
TOSTI: ⎭

MINIMUS: And your own perseverance in the poet's trade after yesterday's discomfiture.

OLLAVE: ⎱
         ⎰ Ay, indeed, sir.
TOSTI: ⎰

MINIMUS: The hound of Heaven closes in for the kill to-day.

OLLAVE: Nae doubt.

TOSTI: Shall we tell him?

OLLAVE: Can he run faster than we, think you?

MINIMUS: Hm?

TOSTI: He would not run, my friend. The poet's trade is above all purely national considerations.

OLLAVE: Ay, defeat is as indifferent to him as victory. Forbye the man's hurdies would present as braw a target tae our cummocks as his——

MINIMUS: What do you mutter, gentlemen?

[*They giggle.*

MINIMUS: Look you, gentlemen. I would not have supposed the chastisement of Satan should so divert you. The brave Cymry, *Gwyr y Gogledd*, even now are they——

[TOSTI *and the* OLLAVE *explode with mirth.*

OLLAVE: It is like this, sir. The gash and wily King of Jutland has got new and caller men to fight for him.

TOSTI: Ay, sir, dead men.

OLLAVE: We were but wishful we might behold the gruntles of the brave Cymry——

TOSTI: *Gwyr y Gogledd!*

OLLAVE: —ay, *Gwyr y Gogledd*, when they charge upon the exposed flank, out-ower there, do you see, nay, more westlins, yont the rash-buss and the birk?

TOSTI: Those quiet and silent ones, with the crows already sitting on their shoulders to peck out British eyes.

MINIMUS: You mean——?

OLLAVE: Ay, to-day you'll need to alter your crambo-jingle and rules of versification. For you'll neer cynghanedd the astonishment that——

TOSTI: The right note of superstition horror——

OLLAVE: —this cantraip slight. . . .

MINIMUS: Gentlemen. . . .

TOSTI:  
⎫ Sir?  
OLLAVE: ⎭

MINIMUS: I shall, if I may, retire.

OLLAVE: Nay, sir, you remain with us. Afterwards you shall entertain the queen—and forbye the young King of Jutland—in chains.

TOSTI: Watch him. These Britons have no doubt a way of suddenly running for it like the rabbits who live with them among the dilapidated stones.

[*But now we hear the trampling of hooves as the Britons charge. "Allelujah" changes to cries of dismay as they find themselves face to face with corpses. Audible too is the clamour of crows. Then the approaching charge of Picts and Danes on the flank of the Britons, the yell of women warriors, the skirling of pipes. The orchestra gathers up these sounds to a triumphant conclusion, and then we hear* MINIMUS, *alone, sadly harping on the hill. An owl hoots. A herd of swine break from the undergrowth. A young pig detaches itself and roots at* MINIMUS' *feet.*

MINIMUS: *Oian a parchellan, a parchell dedwit!*
Listen, o little pig, thou happy little pig!
Bury not thy snout on the top of the mountain.
Burrow in a secluded part of the woods.
The hunting dogs of the Pict and Dane will be after thee
And after Minimus.

Pigling, let us make away together
Before the ninth wave rolls over Catraeth, drowns
Another Gwaelod.

Little pig, I sleep badly
Because of the tumult of grief which is upon me.
Balant is gone to the black glebe.
Beneath a green turf he lies.
I have seen fulfilled the prophecy of the astrologers
When there came over the salt streams men totally
    covered in armour,
War-horses, under them and with two faces.

There is ploughing without reaping.
I predict round Caer Sidi
Seven hundred ships in a north wind
And a wolf in the holy places

Listen, o little pig, thou pig of peace!
My cloak is thin.
Thou stout-armed little one, thou brawny pig!
Nay, tremble not, piggy.
Yet sleep not in the morning, burrow not on the hill.

The hearth of the Brython lay desolate to-night
In the hall of mead and the loquacious drunkard.
Nettles will cover it, greensward lie over it,
Slender brambles, dock-leaves, a crowd of ants.
It will be scratched up by the fowl.
Your brother swine shall root in it.
More accustomed it was to bright torches,
Liquor of wine and bragget, bright yellow,
And burning wood.

Nay, listen to the voice of the water-birds
And strenuous sea-bird. Wonderful it is,
This world is never long in the same condition.
The time is come of the closed, ungenerous hand,
Minstrels out at the door.
A youth will have his own opinion.
Yet listen, little pig, are not the buds of thorns
Very green, the mountains beautiful and beautiful the
    land?

Little pig, it is broad daylight.
Listen.
For me, I will not hear these loud notes,
I will not listen to the birds' tumultuous scream.

Thin is the hair of my head, my covering is not warm.
The dales are my barn, my corn by no means plenteous.
Balant is dead, *mur menwyd*.
We'll take the road south together, piggy *bach*.
The north has been poisoned by rovers
Of a livid, hateful hue and form
Of the race of Adam the ancient.

Pig of Ceridwen, cauldron of inspiration,
*Oian a parchellan, a parchell dedwit.* . . .

----

A Singer: His throat long parched on breeze and brine,
Oft will a roving Dane repine
For Jutland ale or British mead
And half a horn of Rhenish wine.
(There's Jutland ale, there's British mead,
There's harp and hall, there's fire and wine. . . .)

Fyris: There are no cliffs in Jutland?

Hamlet: No, that thin black line is all our coast. And
that too is first ground to sand by the grey-haired
tempests of Ægir and afterwards washed away.

Hermintrude: It is washed to Britain. So do these three
kingdoms become one indeed. But there is more of
Denmark?

Hamlet: Yes, there are islands beyond, of which the
chief is Zealand——

Hermintrude: Where the high king lives?

Hamlet: Ay, Wiglek, the new tyrant.

HERMINTRUDE: Ah!

FYRIS: And there are to be new wars, Hamlet?

HAMLET: First I shall pay tribute to Wiglek. Then I shall drive out Fjalar. Afterwards . . .

HERMINTRUDE: What?

FYRIS: Afterwards——?

HAMLET: We shall see.

HERMINTRUDE: What kind of man is the high king?

THE SINGER: Upon the oar his fingers bleed,
Hoarsely the heart cries out its need
To kill and drink, to kiss, to dine
And sail away without a sign.
(He'll sing, he'll brag, he'll murder and breed,
He'll leave the harbour full indeed,
He'll lose the land where he sank his greed
And sail away without a sign. . . .)

———————————

GERTRUDE: And so we are the four who have loved Hamlet?

TOSTI: Nay, there are more than you.

THORA: The four women.

HERMINTRUDE: Three of whom stand to-day in tears, as though the battle were already lost.

FYRIS: Nay, I do not weep.

TOSTI: These armies are very ill-matched.

HERMINTRUDE: Could Hamlet in honour refuse battle?

GERTRUDE: No.

THORA: No, he could not refuse, not after the death of Fjalar.

HERMINTRUDE: Have I not sworn that, if he is killed, I will follow him into——

GERTRUDE: Into what?

THORA: There are no women in Valhalla, not even Pictish queens.

HERMINTRUDE: Then I will be the first.

FYRIS: Into Heaven. . . .

THORA: Here is Drafnar.

DRAFNAR: Ladies——

GERTRUDE: How does the battle go, Drafnar?

DRAFNAR: Ill, lady. They have turned my wing.

HERMINTRUDE: Then get you outside and fight again, man.

DRAFNAR: I came to see whether any of you desire conduct to another place. The king was more especially troubled about yourself, Queen of Picts.

THORA: Well he might be. She is conqueror's spoils.

GERTRUDE: I stay.

FYRIS: I await my husband.

THORA: I stay.

HERMINTRUDE: I, too, stay.

DRAFNAR: I will tell the king. Now I will go and build another rampart of dead about me.

GERTRUDE: Is Hamlet hurt?

FYRIS: How is my lord?

THORA: How is Hamlet?

DRAFNAR: The king is unhurt. I think he tires a little. They are all about him. But I go.

GERTRUDE: A lack of hope was set on Hamlet's face.

THORA: And now on Drafnar's.

FYRIS: Lord God of Hosts, be over Amleth with thy wing.

TOSTI: I saw the fall of Fjalar, I shall see Hamlet follow. In the acre of the undying, they will eye each other And ask what set them at war in this mid-world.

HERMINTRUDE: You too croak doom, old frog.

TOSTI: I will dance a jig for you lady.

HERMINTRUDE: And you, my corbie, why do you not sing?

OLLAVE: My strings are split with damp, great queen.

HERMINTRUDE: Since it is I of you all whom the king loves——

FYRIS: We shall not boast of Amleth's love, lady, but of our own.

GERTRUDE: I bore him, and for a year I wove threads together to help him to his revenge. And this girl with me.

FYRIS: I still enjoy his son.

THORA: I held him second in my arms, first as a man. I have no child of his, but to make me betray him they thumbed blood from my nipples, calling it a trial. I fed with my breast his famished enemies.

HERMINTRUDE: I gave him a kingdom.

FYRIS: He is my kingdom. I gave him my father and my father's kingdom. I retain my God.

GERTRUDE: Speak, Tosti.

TOSTI: A man is worthier than a word, but the word endures.
I dressed his nakedness with the saga's statement.
The dead are easily pleased, they do not complain of the fit.

*[A flourish, distant.*

HERMINTRUDE: What noise is that?

THORA: I see men coming.

FYRIS: Lord God of Hosts!

GERTRUDE: It is Wiglek.

HERMINTRUDE: He strides among them like the sun dancing at Easter.

WIGLEK: Which is his queen?

FYRIS: I am, my lord.

WIGLEK: Nay, not the King of Britain's daughter. His queen.

HERMINTRUDE: I am here, King of Denmark.

WIGLEK: Ah!

GERTRUDE: And my son, Wiglek?

WIGLEK: Hamlet is——

FYRIS:
⎫
⎬ No!
THORA:
⎭

TOSTI: The tree is split! His blood has rinsed his armour clean!

GERTRUDE: So you have killed him.

WIGLEK: They are bringing him in on his shield, Gertrude.

OLLAVE: This story begins and ends with a shield.

THORA: Is there a corner left on it for his death?

GERTRUDE: This story begins and ends with parricide.

WIGLEK: Sister!

TOSTI: It ends with a queen's betrayal——

GERTRUDE: How so?

THORA: A queen's betrayal, that's certain.

HERMINTRUDE: What, fellow?

FYRIS: It is so indeed.

TOSTI: —as it began.

GERTRUDE: Ah, Tosti!

THORA: What are you waiting for, Hermintrude? He has fought for you and won.

WIGLEK: Quiet, girl, or I——

HERMINTRUDE: I do not know the laws of this country, Wiglek. But they say I am conqueror's spoils.

WIGLEK (*under the spell*): If it is your own will, lady——

HERMINTRUDE: Speak, my tongue.

OLLAVE: Let us honour all women and among them
    queens.
They gave us birth, they give us
The only pleasure that is worth having,
And at the end they'll wash us for the grave.

TOSTI: He is coming.

[*Funeral drums approach, a crowd following.*

OLLAVE: I am sorrowful at my queen's fickleness.
Her first king, Hamlet, was a great hero.
But so it is written, so it is written down.
It is the nature of the moon to change,
Pulling the tide of hearts this way and that.

TOSTI: Let none rail against fate, none fuss.
The design is seen only as we unwind it.

DRAFNAR: Bear my blood-brother gently.

TOSTI:                   O tender Drafnar!

WOMEN: Bear him gently. This was a great hero.

TOSTI: Let all his runes cry out, his lovers speak.

FYRIS: Child in my arms, him you might have chidden.

GERTRUDE: Child gone from my arms, chilling and
    chafed without me.

THORA: Man in my arms and the quick look of thankfulness.

HERMINTRUDE: Man, from my arms death weaned you once and for all.

WOMEN: Man on a shield——

MEN: A tale on fell and foss
We told with him.

WOMEN: Man on a shield, we follow.

MEN: Man on a shield——

WOMEN: A tale of laughter and loss
We watched unfold.

MEN: Man on a shield, lie still.